Is It Autism or OCD?

Stims, Rituals, Special Interests and Intrusive Thoughts, and How to Tell Which Is Which

Decoding the Overlap · Book 2

Evie Dove Huynh

This book is for general educational and informational purposes. It is not a diagnostic instrument and is not a substitute for individualized medical, psychological, psychiatric, or other professional care.
No specific result is promised. Decisions about assessment, treatment, medication, exposure-based work, accommodations, or other supports should be made with appropriately qualified professionals who can consider your full history and circumstances.
The names and scenarios in this book are composites created to illustrate common patterns. They are not intended to identify, portray, harm, or misrepresent any specific person or organization.

ISBN: 978-1-911838-63-0

Table of Contents

Preface

Autism and obsessive-compulsive disorder are both associated with forms of repetition, but repetition is not a diagnosis. Autism can involve repetitive movements, focused interests, routines, a preference for sameness, and sensory differences. OCD can involve repetitive behavior and mental acts that a person feels driven to perform in response to intrusive thoughts, feared consequences, doubt, or rigid rules. The overlap is clinically important because the outside shape of a behavior can conceal a different internal function.

That distinction is the central subject of this book. It uses the Four-Clue Overlap Map, a plain-language method for examining trigger, function, interruption, and history. The map does not turn self-observation into diagnosis. It helps you describe a pattern with enough precision that a clinician can ask better questions.

The gap this book addresses appears before treatment. Reader-facing material often explains autism after autism has been identified, or OCD after OCD has been identified. Clinician manuals discuss differential diagnosis and treatment adaptation, but many adults are still trying to work out why one explanation fits some experiences and fails to explain others. They may also have received treatment that helped one part of the picture while leaving another untouched.

This book lays common points of confusion side by side. It looks at stims and compulsions, routines and rituals, special interests and obsessions, sameness and certainty, sensory distress and fear, intrusive thoughts, mental rituals, co-occurrence, treatment fit, and assessment preparation. It also explains why treatment should be aimed at the mechanism it is meant to change. ERP is an established OCD treatment, and research supports adapted CBT for some autistic people with co-occurring OCD. That is different from using exposure to suppress a useful autistic regulation strategy.

This is Book 2 in the Decoding the Overlap series, a series for questions that come before diagnosis. The primary audience is adults who have been given one explanation and still have unresolved questions about the other. Family members and partners may also find the comparisons useful, especially when outward behavior has been interpreted too quickly.

This book provides general educational information. It cannot diagnose autism, OCD, or any other condition, and it does not replace a full assessment or individualized treatment plan. If symptoms are causing marked distress, taking substantial time, interfering with daily life, or creating safety concerns, seek qualified professional help. The purpose here is simpler: to give you a clearer vocabulary for the question you are already trying to ask.

Introduction The Question Before the Label

Two conditions can share a visible behavior while asking for different clinical questions. Autism can include repetitive movements, strong interests, routines, a preference for sameness, and sensory differences. OCD can include repetitive behavior too, but it is defined around obsessions, compulsions, or both. The overlap creates a practical problem for people whose lived experience does not fit neatly into one label.

This book begins before diagnosis. It is not a self-test and it does not ask you to choose a side. It teaches a method for describing patterns in a way that is more useful than appearance alone. The method is called the Four-Clue Overlap Map: trigger, function, interruption, and history.

You will use the map across the distinctions people actually struggle with: stims and compulsions, routines and rituals, special interests and obsessions, sensory avoidance and fear avoidance, need for sameness and need for certainty, and ordinary mental repetition versus OCD mental rituals. Later chapters cover co-occurrence, treatment fit, and assessment preparation.

A key caution runs through the book. Exposure and response prevention, usually called ERP, is an evidence-based treatment for OCD. Autistic people with co-occurring OCD can benefit from adapted CBT that includes ERP. That does not justify treating every repetitive autistic behavior as a compulsion. The target matters.

You do not need to arrive at the last page with a diagnosis. A useful outcome is smaller and more realistic: you can describe what is happening, what remains uncertain, and what you want a qualified clinician to examine.

Chapter 1 Two Reasons Repetition Happens

Maya repeats the same short video after work because the rhythm settles her body. She worries that a therapist will call the repetition a compulsion. The outside view is simple: repetition. The inside story is not. A movement, question, sequence, or thought can be repeated for several reasons, and those reasons matter more than the photograph of the behavior. This chapter uses a composite scenario. Maya's details are blended from common patterns described in the literature and are not a portrait of one real person.

Autism and OCD can both include repetition. Autism is defined in part by restricted or repetitive patterns of behavior, interests, or activities, while OCD involves obsessions, compulsions, or both (National Institute of Mental Health [NIMH], n.d.-a; National Institute of Mental Health [NIMH], n.d.-b). That overlap is exactly why appearance is a poor shortcut. The useful question is not simply, 'Is it repetitive?' It is, 'What job is the repetition doing?'

The Chapter Principle

Use the Four-Clue Overlap Map: trigger, function, interruption, and history. For repetitive behavior, an autism-related pattern may be connected with soothing, regulation, interest, or predictability. An OCD pattern is more likely when the act is recruited for preventing or neutralizing a feared outcome. None of these clues diagnoses anything by itself. Together they make a better clinical conversation.

Clue One Trigger

Start with what comes immediately before the behavior. A sensory demand, sudden transition, boredom, excitement, or need for focus can point toward regulation or predictability. A spike of doubt, contamination fear, moral fear, harm image, or 'what if' question can

point toward an OCD cycle. The same person can have both. The goal is to describe the sequence without deciding the label first.

Write the trigger as a camera could record it. 'The plan changed five minutes before we left' is better than 'I was triggered.' 'I noticed a thought that I might have left the stove on' is better than 'My anxiety got bad.' Concrete language lets a clinician ask the next question. Research comparing autism and OCD supports careful attention to phenomenology rather than assuming repetitive acts are equivalent (Cath et al., 2008; Santore et al., 2020).

Clue Two Function

Function means what the behavior is trying to change. Does it add useful sensation, organize attention, reduce overload, preserve a preferred pattern, or make an activity enjoyable? Those are different from trying to cancel danger, prove innocence, remove doubt, achieve a protective feeling, or satisfy a rule that says something bad will happen otherwise. In practice, mixed motives are common. You do not need a perfectly clean answer.

Ask a harder question: if there were no feared consequence at all, would you still want to do it? If the answer is yes because the act feels good, helps concentration, supports transition, or is part of a valued interest, that is information. If the answer is no, and the act feels like a tax paid to reduce threat or doubt, that is different information. Qualitative research with autistic adults who also have OCD describes how difficult and important this distinction can be (Long et al., 2024; Wikramanayake et al., 2018).

Clue Three Interruption

Interruption is not a morality test. Notice what kind of distress appears when the pattern is blocked. Sensory discomfort, disorganization, loss of focus, frustration at abrupt change, or a feeling of being neurologically overloaded can occur around autistic routines and

repetitive behavior. OCD interruption more often exposes the feared uncertainty the compulsion was managing: 'What if I did not check enough?' 'What if the contamination spreads?' 'What if this thought means I am dangerous?'

There is overlap here too. Autistic people can feel intense anxiety when a routine is interrupted, and people with OCD can describe bodily discomfort or a 'not just right' feeling rather than a clear catastrophic belief. That is why one clue never settles the question. The pattern across all four clues is more informative than any single answer.

Clue Four History

History asks when the pattern began and what else was true at the time. Autism is developmental, so a clinician assessing autism looks for a broader developmental pattern, not only current repetition. OCD can begin in childhood, adolescence, or adulthood and may wax and wane. A new ritual appearing after a period of intrusive doubt tells a different story from a lifelong preference for the same sensory input or sequence. Population and clinic studies show meaningful co-occurrence, so history should leave room for both rather than forcing an either-or answer (Meier et al., 2015; Wikramanayake et al., 2018).

If you can, collect examples from more than one age and setting. Old school reports, family recollections, childhood interests, early sensory patterns, and previous treatment responses can all be useful. Family memory is imperfect, and lack of documentation does not prove absence. Treat it as evidence to discuss, not a verdict.

A Worked Comparison

Take Maya's situation and write two competing explanations. Explanation A: the behavior is mainly connected with soothing, regulation, interest, or predictability. Explanation B: the behavior is mainly connected with preventing or neutralizing a feared outcome.

Now ask what each explanation predicts. If A is closer, accommodation or regulation may reduce distress without requiring the person to defeat a fear. If B is closer, reducing compulsive responding to feared uncertainty may be clinically relevant. If both predictions fit at different times, co-occurrence becomes a serious possibility.

This method prevents a common reasoning error: treating the name of an action as if it revealed its function. 'Checking,' 'repeating,' 'collecting,' 'researching,' and 'avoiding' are verbs, not diagnoses. A person can research a favorite topic for pleasure, research a feared disease for reassurance, or do both in the same evening. Ask what happened before, what the act was supposed to accomplish, and what happened after.

What Treatment Response Can Tell You

Treatment response is information, but it is not a home diagnostic test. ERP is an evidence-based component of CBT for OCD, and studies suggest adapted CBT can help autistic people who genuinely have co-occurring OCD (Russell et al., 2013; Flygare et al., 2020; National Institute for Health and Care Excellence [NICE], 2005/2019). That does not mean every repetitive autistic behavior should be targeted with exposure. If the target is sensory regulation, communication support, or a stable routine rather than an OCD compulsion, removing it can increase distress without treating the problem you meant to treat.

The safer principle is target accuracy. A clinician should identify the feared prediction or compulsive rule before asking you to resist a behavior as part of ERP. Adaptations may include clearer structure, concrete language, slower pacing, attention to sensory needs, and explicit differentiation between OCD goals and autism-related supports. If treatment repeatedly feels aimed at the wrong mechanism, bring that observation back to the clinician rather than trying to push through on principle.

What Appearance Gets Wrong

A quick label can hide mixed functions. With repetitive behavior, three mistakes are especially common. The first is assuming that visible anxiety proves OCD. A disrupted autistic routine or sensory overload can produce intense anxiety without a compulsion being present. The second is assuming that enjoyment rules OCD out. A person can feel temporary relief after a compulsion, and relief can be mistaken for preference. The third is assuming that a behavior has one function forever. A lifelong routine can later become entangled with OCD, or a person can begin using a familiar autistic behavior as part of a new threat-reduction rule.

For that reason, describe episodes rather than traits whenever you can. Instead of writing, "I always do this because I am autistic," record one recent example. Instead of writing, "This is definitely OCD," record the feared possibility, the rule, and what the behavior was supposed to prevent. Good differential assessment is built from patterns across examples. It is also allowed to end with more than one explanation.

Questions to Take to a Clinician

Bring examples instead of conclusions. Useful questions include: 'What makes you think this behavior is a compulsion rather than a regulating repetitive behavior?' 'What feared outcome or uncertainty are we targeting?' 'How are you accounting for sensory needs and developmental history?' 'Could both autism and OCD be present?' 'How will we know whether this intervention is reducing OCD rather than simply increasing my tolerance of distress from losing a useful support?'

A good assessment is not a debate you have to win. It is a process of making the evidence visible. You can help by naming the sequence precisely: what happened, what you thought or sensed, what you did,

what you hoped the act would change, and what happened next. That gives a clinician something more useful than a checklist score alone.

Try the Four-Clue Overlap Map

Choose one example of repetitive behavior. On one page, make four headings: Trigger, Function, Interruption, History. Under Trigger, record what came first. Under Function, record what the behavior was meant to change. Under Interruption, record the kind of distress that appears if you stop. Under History, record when the pattern first appeared and whether it has changed. Add a final line called 'What I am not sure about.' That last line is often the most useful one to bring to assessment.

Principles to Remember

The visible behavior is the beginning of the question, not the answer. For repetitive behavior, look at trigger, function, interruption, and history before assigning meaning. Autism-related repetition can be valuable, regulating, pleasurable, or stabilizing. OCD compulsions are typically recruited into a cycle of threat, doubt, or rule-driven relief. Some experiences sit between those descriptions, and some people have both conditions. Your task is not to diagnose yourself from one clue. It is to build a clearer account of what is happening so the right professional questions can be asked.

References

National Institute of Mental Health. (n.d.-a). Autism spectrum disorder. https://www.nimh.nih.gov/health/publications/autism-spectrum-disorder

National Institute of Mental Health. (n.d.-b). Obsessive-compulsive disorder. https://www.nimh.nih.gov/health/topics/obsessive-compulsive-disorder-ocd

Cath, D. C., Ran, N., Smit, J. H., van Balkom, A. J. L. M., & Comijs, H. C. (2008). Symptom overlap between autism spectrum disorder, generalized social anxiety disorder and obsessive-compulsive disorder in adults: A preliminary case-controlled study. Psychopathology, 41(2), 101-110. https://pubmed.ncbi.nlm.nih.gov/18033980/

Santore, L. A., Gerber, A. H., Gioia, A. N., Bianchi, R., Talledo, F., Peris, T. S., & Lerner, M. D. (2020). Felt but not seen: Observed restricted repetitive behaviors are associated with self-report but not parent-report obsessive-compulsive disorder symptoms in youth with autism. Autism, 24(4), 983-994. https://pmc.ncbi.nlm.nih.gov/articles/PMC7337249/

Long, H. A., Rodgers, J., & South, M. (2024). 'Autism is the arena and OCD is the lion': Autistic adults' experiences of co-occurring obsessive-compulsive disorder. Autism. https://pmc.ncbi.nlm.nih.gov/articles/PMC11497754/

Wikramanayake, W. N. M., Mandy, W., Shahper, S., Kaur, S., Kolli, S., Osman, S., Reid, J., Jefferies-Sewell, K., & Fineberg, N. A. (2018). Autism spectrum disorders in adult outpatients with obsessive compulsive disorder in the UK. International Journal of Psychiatry in Clinical Practice, 22(1), 54-62. https://pubmed.ncbi.nlm.nih.gov/28705096/

Meier, S. M., Petersen, L., Schendel, D. E., Mattheisen, M., Mortensen, P. B., & Mors, O. (2015). Obsessive-compulsive disorder and autism spectrum disorders: Longitudinal and offspring risk. PLOS ONE, 10(11), e0141703. https://pubmed.ncbi.nlm.nih.gov/26558765/

Russell, A. J., Jassi, A., Fullana, M. A., Mack, H., Johnston, K., Heyman, I., Murphy, D. G., & Mataix-Cols, D. (2013). Cognitive behavior therapy for comorbid obsessive-compulsive disorder in high-functioning autism spectrum disorders: A randomized controlled trial. Depression and Anxiety, 30(8), 697-708. https://pubmed.ncbi.nlm.nih.gov/23389964/

Flygare, O., Andersson, E., Ringberg, H., Hellstadius, K., Edbacken, J., Enander, J., Ljotsson, B., Mataix-Cols, D., & Serlachius,

E. (2020). Adapted cognitive behavior therapy for obsessive-compulsive disorder with co-occurring autism spectrum disorder: A clinical effectiveness study. Autism, 24(1), 190-199. https://pubmed.ncbi.nlm.nih.gov/31187645/

National Institute for Health and Care Excellence. (2005, surveillance updated 2019). Obsessive-compulsive disorder and body dysmorphic disorder: Treatment (CG31). https://www.nice.org.uk/guidance/cg31

Chapter 2 Start With Function

The same action can keep its shape while its reason changes. Jonah checks the front door several times. Sometimes he is following a familiar leaving routine. On other days he is trying to make an unbearable doubt disappear. The outside view is simple: repetition. The inside story is not. A movement, question, sequence, or thought can be repeated for several reasons, and those reasons matter more than the photograph of the behavior. This chapter uses a composite scenario. Jonah's details are blended from common patterns described in the literature and are not a portrait of one real person.

Autism and OCD can both include repetition. Autism is defined in part by restricted or repetitive patterns of behavior, interests, or activities, while OCD involves obsessions, compulsions, or both (National Institute of Mental Health [NIMH], n.d.-a; National Institute of Mental Health [NIMH], n.d.-b). That overlap is exactly why appearance is a poor shortcut. The useful question is not simply, 'Is it repetitive?' It is, 'What job is the repetition doing?'

The Chapter Principle

Use the Four-Clue Overlap Map: trigger, function, interruption, and history. For the same outward act, an autism-related pattern may be connected with what the behavior does for the person's nervous system, attention, or enjoyment. An OCD pattern is more likely when the act is recruited for what the behavior is meant to prevent, cancel, check, or make certain. None of these clues diagnoses anything by itself. Together they make a better clinical conversation.

Clue One Trigger

Start with what comes immediately before the behavior. A sensory demand, sudden transition, boredom, excitement, or need for focus can point toward regulation or predictability. A spike of doubt,

contamination fear, moral fear, harm image, or 'what if' question can point toward an OCD cycle. The same person can have both. The goal is to describe the sequence without deciding the label first.

Write the trigger as a camera could record it. 'The plan changed five minutes before we left' is better than 'I was triggered.' 'I noticed a thought that I might have left the stove on' is better than 'My anxiety got bad.' Concrete language lets a clinician ask the next question. Research comparing autism and OCD supports careful attention to phenomenology rather than assuming repetitive acts are equivalent (Cath et al., 2008; Santore et al., 2020).

Clue Two Function

Function means what the behavior is trying to change. Does it add useful sensation, organize attention, reduce overload, preserve a preferred pattern, or make an activity enjoyable? Those are different from trying to cancel danger, prove innocence, remove doubt, achieve a protective feeling, or satisfy a rule that says something bad will happen otherwise. In practice, mixed motives are common. You do not need a perfectly clean answer.

Ask a harder question: if there were no feared consequence at all, would you still want to do it? If the answer is yes because the act feels good, helps concentration, supports transition, or is part of a valued interest, that is information. If the answer is no, and the act feels like a tax paid to reduce threat or doubt, that is different information. Qualitative research with autistic adults who also have OCD describes how difficult and important this distinction can be (Long et al., 2024; Wikramanayake et al., 2018).

Clue Three Interruption

Interruption is not a morality test. Notice what kind of distress appears when the pattern is blocked. Sensory discomfort, disorganization, loss of focus, frustration at abrupt change, or a feeling of being

neurologically overloaded can occur around autistic routines and repetitive behavior. OCD interruption more often exposes the feared uncertainty the compulsion was managing: 'What if I did not check enough?' 'What if the contamination spreads?' 'What if this thought means I am dangerous?'

There is overlap here too. Autistic people can feel intense anxiety when a routine is interrupted, and people with OCD can describe bodily discomfort or a 'not just right' feeling rather than a clear catastrophic belief. That is why one clue never settles the question. The pattern across all four clues is more informative than any single answer.

Clue Four History

History asks when the pattern began and what else was true at the time. Autism is developmental, so a clinician assessing autism looks for a broader developmental pattern, not only current repetition. OCD can begin in childhood, adolescence, or adulthood and may wax and wane. A new ritual appearing after a period of intrusive doubt tells a different story from a lifelong preference for the same sensory input or sequence. Population and clinic studies show meaningful co-occurrence, so history should leave room for both rather than forcing an either-or answer (Meier et al., 2015; Wikramanayake et al., 2018).

If you can, collect examples from more than one age and setting. Old school reports, family recollections, childhood interests, early sensory patterns, and previous treatment responses can all be useful. Family memory is imperfect, and lack of documentation does not prove absence. Treat it as evidence to discuss, not a verdict.

A Worked Comparison

Take Jonah's situation and write two competing explanations. Explanation A: the behavior is mainly connected with what the behavior does for the person's nervous system, attention, or enjoyment.

Explanation B: the behavior is mainly connected with what the behavior is meant to prevent, cancel, check, or make certain. Now ask what each explanation predicts. If A is closer, accommodation or regulation may reduce distress without requiring the person to defeat a fear. If B is closer, reducing compulsive responding to feared uncertainty may be clinically relevant. If both predictions fit at different times, co-occurrence becomes a serious possibility.

This method prevents a common reasoning error: treating the name of an action as if it revealed its function. 'Checking,' 'repeating,' 'collecting,' 'researching,' and 'avoiding' are verbs, not diagnoses. A person can research a favorite topic for pleasure, research a feared disease for reassurance, or do both in the same evening. Ask what happened before, what the act was supposed to accomplish, and what happened after.

What Treatment Response Can Tell You

Treatment response is information, but it is not a home diagnostic test. ERP is an evidence-based component of CBT for OCD, and studies suggest adapted CBT can help autistic people who genuinely have co-occurring OCD (Russell et al., 2013; Flygare et al., 2020; National Institute for Health and Care Excellence [NICE], 2005/2019). That does not mean every repetitive autistic behavior should be targeted with exposure. If the target is sensory regulation, communication support, or a stable routine rather than an OCD compulsion, removing it can increase distress without treating the problem you meant to treat.

The safer principle is target accuracy. A clinician should identify the feared prediction or compulsive rule before asking you to resist a behavior as part of ERP. Adaptations may include clearer structure, concrete language, slower pacing, attention to sensory needs, and explicit differentiation between OCD goals and autism-related supports. If treatment repeatedly feels aimed at the wrong mechanism, bring that observation back to the clinician rather than trying to push through on principle.

What Appearance Gets Wrong

A quick label can hide mixed functions. With the same outward act, three mistakes are especially common. The first is assuming that visible anxiety proves OCD. A disrupted autistic routine or sensory overload can produce intense anxiety without a compulsion being present. The second is assuming that enjoyment rules OCD out. A person can feel temporary relief after a compulsion, and relief can be mistaken for preference. The third is assuming that a behavior has one function forever. A lifelong routine can later become entangled with OCD, or a person can begin using a familiar autistic behavior as part of a new threat-reduction rule.

For that reason, describe episodes rather than traits whenever you can. Instead of writing, "I always do this because I am autistic," record one recent example. Instead of writing, "This is definitely OCD," record the feared possibility, the rule, and what the behavior was supposed to prevent. Good differential assessment is built from patterns across examples. It is also allowed to end with more than one explanation.

Questions to Take to a Clinician

Bring examples instead of conclusions. Useful questions include: 'What makes you think this behavior is a compulsion rather than a regulating repetitive behavior?' 'What feared outcome or uncertainty are we targeting?' 'How are you accounting for sensory needs and developmental history?' 'Could both autism and OCD be present?' 'How will we know whether this intervention is reducing OCD rather than simply increasing my tolerance of distress from losing a useful support?'

A good assessment is not a debate you have to win. It is a process of making the evidence visible. You can help by naming the sequence precisely: what happened, what you thought or sensed, what you did,

what you hoped the act would change, and what happened next. That gives a clinician something more useful than a checklist score alone.

Try the Four-Clue Overlap Map

Choose one example of the same outward act. On one page, make four headings: Trigger, Function, Interruption, History. Under Trigger, record what came first. Under Function, record what the behavior was meant to change. Under Interruption, record the kind of distress that appears if you stop. Under History, record when the pattern first appeared and whether it has changed. Add a final line called 'What I am not sure about.' That last line is often the most useful one to bring to assessment.

In a Nutshell

The visible behavior is the beginning of the question, not the answer. For the same outward act, look at trigger, function, interruption, and history before assigning meaning. Autism-related repetition can be valuable, regulating, pleasurable, or stabilizing. OCD compulsions are typically recruited into a cycle of threat, doubt, or rule-driven relief. Some experiences sit between those descriptions, and some people have both conditions. Your task is not to diagnose yourself from one clue. It is to build a clearer account of what is happening so the right professional questions can be asked.

References

National Institute of Mental Health. (n.d.-a). Autism spectrum disorder. https://www.nimh.nih.gov/health/publications/autism-spectrum-disorder

National Institute of Mental Health. (n.d.-b). Obsessive-compulsive disorder. https://www.nimh.nih.gov/health/topics/obsessive-compulsive-disorder-ocd

Cath, D. C., Ran, N., Smit, J. H., van Balkom, A. J. L. M., & Comijs, H. C. (2008). Symptom overlap between autism spectrum disorder, generalized social anxiety disorder and obsessive-compulsive disorder in adults: A preliminary case-controlled study. Psychopathology, 41(2), 101-110. https://pubmed.ncbi.nlm.nih.gov/18033980/

Santore, L. A., Gerber, A. H., Gioia, A. N., Bianchi, R., Talledo, F., Peris, T. S., & Lerner, M. D. (2020). Felt but not seen: Observed restricted repetitive behaviors are associated with self-report but not parent-report obsessive-compulsive disorder symptoms in youth with autism. Autism, 24(4), 983-994. https://pmc.ncbi.nlm.nih.gov/articles/PMC7337249/

Long, H. A., Rodgers, J., & South, M. (2024). 'Autism is the arena and OCD is the lion': Autistic adults' experiences of co-occurring obsessive-compulsive disorder. Autism. https://pmc.ncbi.nlm.nih.gov/articles/PMC11497754/

Wikramanayake, W. N. M., Mandy, W., Shahper, S., Kaur, S., Kolli, S., Osman, S., Reid, J., Jefferies-Sewell, K., & Fineberg, N. A. (2018). Autism spectrum disorders in adult outpatients with obsessive compulsive disorder in the UK. International Journal of Psychiatry in Clinical Practice, 22(1), 54-62. https://pubmed.ncbi.nlm.nih.gov/28705096/

Meier, S. M., Petersen, L., Schendel, D. E., Mattheisen, M., Mortensen, P. B., & Mors, O. (2015). Obsessive-compulsive disorder and autism spectrum disorders: Longitudinal and offspring risk. PLOS ONE, 10(11), e0141703. https://pubmed.ncbi.nlm.nih.gov/26558765/

Russell, A. J., Jassi, A., Fullana, M. A., Mack, H., Johnston, K., Heyman, I., Murphy, D. G., & Mataix-Cols, D. (2013). Cognitive behavior therapy for comorbid obsessive-compulsive disorder in high-functioning autism spectrum disorders: A randomized controlled trial. Depression and Anxiety, 30(8), 697-708. https://pubmed.ncbi.nlm.nih.gov/23389964/

Flygare, O., Andersson, E., Ringberg, H., Hellstadius, K., Edbacken, J., Enander, J., Ljotsson, B., Mataix-Cols, D., & Serlachius,

E. (2020). Adapted cognitive behavior therapy for obsessive-compulsive disorder with co-occurring autism spectrum disorder: A clinical effectiveness study. Autism, 24(1), 190-199. https://pubmed.ncbi.nlm.nih.gov/31187645/

National Institute for Health and Care Excellence. (2005, surveillance updated 2019). Obsessive-compulsive disorder and body dysmorphic disorder: Treatment (CG31). https://www.nice.org.uk/guidance/cg31

Chapter 3 Stims and Compulsions

Priya rubs two fingertips together during meetings. It becomes faster when the room is loud, but she does not believe anything bad will happen if she stops. The outside view is simple: repetition. The inside story is not. A movement, question, sequence, or thought can be repeated for several reasons, and those reasons matter more than the photograph of the behavior. This chapter uses a composite scenario. Priya's details are blended from common patterns described in the literature and are not a portrait of one real person.

Autism and OCD can both include repetition. Autism is defined in part by restricted or repetitive patterns of behavior, interests, or activities, while OCD involves obsessions, compulsions, or both (National Institute of Mental Health [NIMH], n.d.-a; National Institute of Mental Health [NIMH], n.d.-b). That overlap is exactly why appearance is a poor shortcut. The useful question is not simply, 'Is it repetitive?' It is, 'What job is the repetition doing?'

The Chapter Principle

Use the Four-Clue Overlap Map: trigger, function, interruption, and history. For repetitive movement, an autism-related pattern may be connected with regulation, sensory input, expression, or focus. An OCD pattern is more likely when the act is recruited for fear reduction, neutralization, checking, or rule completion. None of these clues diagnoses anything by itself. Together they make a better clinical conversation.

Clue One Trigger

Start with what comes immediately before the behavior. A sensory demand, sudden transition, boredom, excitement, or need for focus can point toward regulation or predictability. A spike of doubt, contamination fear, moral fear, harm image, or 'what if' question can

point toward an OCD cycle. The same person can have both. The goal is to describe the sequence without deciding the label first.

Write the trigger as a camera could record it. 'The plan changed five minutes before we left' is better than 'I was triggered.' 'I noticed a thought that I might have left the stove on' is better than 'My anxiety got bad.' Concrete language lets a clinician ask the next question. Research comparing autism and OCD supports careful attention to phenomenology rather than assuming repetitive acts are equivalent (Cath et al., 2008; Santore et al., 2020).

Clue Two Function

Function means what the behavior is trying to change. Does it add useful sensation, organize attention, reduce overload, preserve a preferred pattern, or make an activity enjoyable? Those are different from trying to cancel danger, prove innocence, remove doubt, achieve a protective feeling, or satisfy a rule that says something bad will happen otherwise. In practice, mixed motives are common. You do not need a perfectly clean answer.

Ask a harder question: if there were no feared consequence at all, would you still want to do it? If the answer is yes because the act feels good, helps concentration, supports transition, or is part of a valued interest, that is information. If the answer is no, and the act feels like a tax paid to reduce threat or doubt, that is different information. Qualitative research with autistic adults who also have OCD describes how difficult and important this distinction can be (Long et al., 2024; Wikramanayake et al., 2018).

Clue Three Interruption

Interruption is not a morality test. Notice what kind of distress appears when the pattern is blocked. Sensory discomfort, disorganization, loss of focus, frustration at abrupt change, or a feeling of being neurologically overloaded can occur around autistic routines and

repetitive behavior. OCD interruption more often exposes the feared uncertainty the compulsion was managing: 'What if I did not check enough?' 'What if the contamination spreads?' 'What if this thought means I am dangerous?'

There is overlap here too. Autistic people can feel intense anxiety when a routine is interrupted, and people with OCD can describe bodily discomfort or a 'not just right' feeling rather than a clear catastrophic belief. That is why one clue never settles the question. The pattern across all four clues is more informative than any single answer.

Clue Four History

History asks when the pattern began and what else was true at the time. Autism is developmental, so a clinician assessing autism looks for a broader developmental pattern, not only current repetition. OCD can begin in childhood, adolescence, or adulthood and may wax and wane. A new ritual appearing after a period of intrusive doubt tells a different story from a lifelong preference for the same sensory input or sequence. Population and clinic studies show meaningful co-occurrence, so history should leave room for both rather than forcing an either-or answer (Meier et al., 2015; Wikramanayake et al., 2018).

If you can, collect examples from more than one age and setting. Old school reports, family recollections, childhood interests, early sensory patterns, and previous treatment responses can all be useful. Family memory is imperfect, and lack of documentation does not prove absence. Treat it as evidence to discuss, not a verdict.

A Worked Comparison

Take Priya's situation and write two competing explanations. Explanation A: the behavior is mainly connected with regulation, sensory input, expression, or focus. Explanation B: the behavior is mainly connected with fear reduction, neutralization, checking, or rule completion. Now ask what each explanation predicts. If A is closer, accommodation or regulation may reduce distress without requiring the person to defeat a fear. If B is closer, reducing compulsive responding to feared uncertainty may be clinically relevant. If both predictions fit at different times, co-occurrence becomes a serious possibility.

This method prevents a common reasoning error: treating the name of an action as if it revealed its function. 'Checking,' 'repeating,' 'collecting,' 'researching,' and 'avoiding' are verbs, not diagnoses. A person can research a favorite topic for pleasure, research a feared disease for reassurance, or do both in the same evening. Ask what happened before, what the act was supposed to accomplish, and what happened after.

What Treatment Response Can Tell You

Treatment response is information, but it is not a home diagnostic test. ERP is an evidence-based component of CBT for OCD, and studies suggest adapted CBT can help autistic people who genuinely have co-occurring OCD (Russell et al., 2013; Flygare et al., 2020; National Institute for Health and Care Excellence [NICE], 2005/2019). That does not mean every repetitive autistic behavior should be targeted with exposure. If the target is sensory regulation, communication support, or a stable routine rather than an OCD compulsion, removing it can increase distress without treating the problem you meant to treat.

The safer principle is target accuracy. A clinician should identify the feared prediction or compulsive rule before asking you to resist a behavior as part of ERP. Adaptations may include clearer structure, concrete language, slower pacing, attention to sensory needs, and explicit differentiation between OCD goals and autism-related supports. If treatment repeatedly feels aimed at the wrong mechanism, bring that observation back to the clinician rather than trying to push through on principle.

What Appearance Gets Wrong

A quick label can hide mixed functions. With repetitive movement, three mistakes are especially common. The first is assuming that visible anxiety proves OCD. A disrupted autistic routine or sensory overload can produce intense anxiety without a compulsion being present. The second is assuming that enjoyment rules OCD out. A person can feel temporary relief after a compulsion, and relief can be mistaken for preference. The third is assuming that a behavior has one function forever. A lifelong routine can later become entangled with OCD, or a person can begin using a familiar autistic behavior as part of a new threat-reduction rule.

For that reason, describe episodes rather than traits whenever you can. Instead of writing, "I always do this because I am autistic," record one recent example. Instead of writing, "This is definitely OCD," record the feared possibility, the rule, and what the behavior was supposed to prevent. Good differential assessment is built from patterns across examples. It is also allowed to end with more than one explanation.

Movement Changes With Context

Stimming is a particularly poor place to use appearance as a diagnostic shortcut because movement is sensitive to context. A person may rock more when concentrating, pace while processing language, flap when excited, rub a texture to stay present in a noisy room, or repeat a movement because it is simply satisfying. The movement may become faster under stress without becoming a fear-neutralizing ritual. Stress changes many useful behaviors.

A compulsion can also be a movement. The difference to investigate is whether the movement has been recruited into a rule about danger, responsibility, contamination, completeness, or certainty. If a hand movement has to be performed exactly eight times because stopping at seven feels as though a family member may be harmed, the feared consequence belongs in the description. If the same hand movement helps the person follow a conversation and there is no protective rule attached, that belongs in the description too.

This matters in assessment because suppressing all visible repetition can remove information. If you force yourself to sit completely still for the appointment, a clinician may not see a regulation strategy you use every day. You do not need to perform a stim on command, but you also do not have to hide it to look credible. Describe when it appears, what it gives you, and whether any separate rule has attached itself to it over time.

Questions to Take to a Clinician

Bring examples instead of conclusions. Useful questions include: 'What makes you think this behavior is a compulsion rather than a regulating repetitive behavior?' 'What feared outcome or uncertainty are we targeting?' 'How are you accounting for sensory needs and developmental history?' 'Could both autism and OCD be present?' 'How will we know whether this intervention is reducing OCD rather than simply increasing my tolerance of distress from losing a useful support?'

A good assessment is not a debate you have to win. It is a process of making the evidence visible. You can help by naming the sequence precisely: what happened, what you thought or sensed, what you did, what you hoped the act would change, and what happened next. That gives a clinician something more useful than a checklist score alone.

Try the Four-Clue Overlap Map

Choose one example of repetitive movement. On one page, make four headings: Trigger, Function, Interruption, History. Under Trigger, record what came first. Under Function, record what the behavior was meant to change. Under Interruption, record the kind of distress that appears if you stop. Under History, record when the pattern first appeared and whether it has changed. Add a final line called 'What I am not sure about.' That last line is often the most useful one to bring to assessment.

Principles to Remember

The visible behavior is the beginning of the question, not the answer. For repetitive movement, look at trigger, function, interruption, and history before assigning meaning. Autism-related repetition can be valuable, regulating, pleasurable, or stabilizing. OCD compulsions are typically recruited into a cycle of threat, doubt, or rule-driven relief. Some experiences sit between those descriptions, and some people have both conditions. Your task is not to diagnose yourself from one clue. It is to build a clearer account of what is happening so the right professional questions can be asked.

References

National Institute of Mental Health. (n.d.-a). Autism spectrum disorder. https://www.nimh.nih.gov/health/publications/autism-spectrum-disorder

National Institute of Mental Health. (n.d.-b). Obsessive-compulsive disorder. https://www.nimh.nih.gov/health/topics/obsessive-compulsive-disorder-ocd

Cath, D. C., Ran, N., Smit, J. H., van Balkom, A. J. L. M., & Comijs, H. C. (2008). Symptom overlap between autism spectrum disorder, generalized social anxiety disorder and obsessive-compulsive disorder in adults: A preliminary case-controlled study. Psychopathology, 41(2), 101-110. https://pubmed.ncbi.nlm.nih.gov/18033980/

Santore, L. A., Gerber, A. H., Gioia, A. N., Bianchi, R., Talledo, F., Peris, T. S., & Lerner, M. D. (2020). Felt but not seen: Observed restricted repetitive behaviors are associated with self-report but not

parent-report obsessive-compulsive disorder symptoms in youth with autism. Autism, 24(4), 983-994. https://pmc.ncbi.nlm.nih.gov/articles/PMC7337249/

Long, H. A., Rodgers, J., & South, M. (2024). 'Autism is the arena and OCD is the lion': Autistic adults' experiences of co-occurring obsessive-compulsive disorder. Autism. https://pmc.ncbi.nlm.nih.gov/articles/PMC11497754/

Wikramanayake, W. N. M., Mandy, W., Shahper, S., Kaur, S., Kolli, S., Osman, S., Reid, J., Jefferies-Sewell, K., & Fineberg, N. A. (2018). Autism spectrum disorders in adult outpatients with obsessive compulsive disorder in the UK. International Journal of Psychiatry in Clinical Practice, 22(1), 54-62. https://pubmed.ncbi.nlm.nih.gov/28705096/

Meier, S. M., Petersen, L., Schendel, D. E., Mattheisen, M., Mortensen, P. B., & Mors, O. (2015). Obsessive-compulsive disorder and autism spectrum disorders: Longitudinal and offspring risk. PLOS ONE, 10(11), e0141703. https://pubmed.ncbi.nlm.nih.gov/26558765/

Russell, A. J., Jassi, A., Fullana, M. A., Mack, H., Johnston, K., Heyman, I., Murphy, D. G., & Mataix-Cols, D. (2013). Cognitive behavior therapy for comorbid obsessive-compulsive disorder in high-functioning autism spectrum disorders: A randomized controlled trial. Depression and Anxiety, 30(8), 697-708. https://pubmed.ncbi.nlm.nih.gov/23389964/

Flygare, O., Andersson, E., Ringberg, H., Hellstadius, K., Edbacken, J., Enander, J., Ljotsson, B., Mataix-Cols, D., & Serlachius, E. (2020). Adapted cognitive behavior therapy for obsessive-compulsive disorder with co-occurring autism spectrum disorder: A clinical effectiveness study. Autism, 24(1), 190-199. https://pubmed.ncbi.nlm.nih.gov/31187645/

National Institute for Health and Care Excellence. (2005, surveillance updated 2019). Obsessive-compulsive disorder and body dysmorphic disorder: Treatment (CG31). https://www.nice.org.uk/guidance/cg31

Chapter 4 Routines and Rituals

A repeated sequence tells you almost nothing until you know what would happen if it changed. Daniel makes breakfast in the same order every weekday. A second sequence appears after he reads a contamination story online, and that one carries a very different kind of urgency. The outside view is simple: repetition. The inside story is not. A movement, question, sequence, or thought can be repeated for several reasons, and those reasons matter more than the photograph of the behavior. This chapter uses a composite scenario. Daniel's details are blended from common patterns described in the literature and are not a portrait of one real person.

Autism and OCD can both include repetition. Autism is defined in part by restricted or repetitive patterns of behavior, interests, or activities, while OCD involves obsessions, compulsions, or both (National Institute of Mental Health [NIMH], n.d.-a; National Institute of Mental Health [NIMH], n.d.-b). That overlap is exactly why appearance is a poor shortcut. The useful question is not simply, 'Is it repetitive?' It is, 'What job is the repetition doing?'

The Chapter Principle

Use the Four-Clue Overlap Map: trigger, function, interruption, and history. For repeated sequences, an autism-related pattern may be connected with predictability, reduced decision load, transition support, or preference. An OCD pattern is more likely when the act is recruited for a rule that must be completed to prevent danger, guilt, contamination, or uncertainty. None of these clues diagnoses anything by itself. Together they make a better clinical conversation.

Clue One Trigger

Start with what comes immediately before the behavior. A sensory demand, sudden transition, boredom, excitement, or need for focus can

point toward regulation or predictability. A spike of doubt, contamination fear, moral fear, harm image, or 'what if' question can point toward an OCD cycle. The same person can have both. The goal is to describe the sequence without deciding the label first.

Write the trigger as a camera could record it. 'The plan changed five minutes before we left' is better than 'I was triggered.' 'I noticed a thought that I might have left the stove on' is better than 'My anxiety got bad.' Concrete language lets a clinician ask the next question. Research comparing autism and OCD supports careful attention to phenomenology rather than assuming repetitive acts are equivalent (Cath et al., 2008; Santore et al., 2020).

Clue Two Function

Function means what the behavior is trying to change. Does it add useful sensation, organize attention, reduce overload, preserve a preferred pattern, or make an activity enjoyable? Those are different from trying to cancel danger, prove innocence, remove doubt, achieve a protective feeling, or satisfy a rule that says something bad will happen otherwise. In practice, mixed motives are common. You do not need a perfectly clean answer.

Ask a harder question: if there were no feared consequence at all, would you still want to do it? If the answer is yes because the act feels good, helps concentration, supports transition, or is part of a valued interest, that is information. If the answer is no, and the act feels like a tax paid to reduce threat or doubt, that is different information. Qualitative research with autistic adults who also have OCD describes how difficult and important this distinction can be (Long et al., 2024; Wikramanayake et al., 2018).

Clue Three Interruption

Interruption is not a morality test. Notice what kind of distress appears when the pattern is blocked. Sensory discomfort, disorganization, loss

of focus, frustration at abrupt change, or a feeling of being neurologically overloaded can occur around autistic routines and repetitive behavior. OCD interruption more often exposes the feared uncertainty the compulsion was managing: 'What if I did not check enough?' 'What if the contamination spreads?' 'What if this thought means I am dangerous?'

There is overlap here too. Autistic people can feel intense anxiety when a routine is interrupted, and people with OCD can describe bodily discomfort or a 'not just right' feeling rather than a clear catastrophic belief. That is why one clue never settles the question. The pattern across all four clues is more informative than any single answer.

Clue Four History

History asks when the pattern began and what else was true at the time. Autism is developmental, so a clinician assessing autism looks for a broader developmental pattern, not only current repetition. OCD can begin in childhood, adolescence, or adulthood and may wax and wane. A new ritual appearing after a period of intrusive doubt tells a different story from a lifelong preference for the same sensory input or sequence. Population and clinic studies show meaningful co-occurrence, so history should leave room for both rather than forcing an either-or answer (Meier et al., 2015; Wikramanayake et al., 2018).

If you can, collect examples from more than one age and setting. Old school reports, family recollections, childhood interests, early sensory patterns, and previous treatment responses can all be useful. Family memory is imperfect, and lack of documentation does not prove absence. Treat it as evidence to discuss, not a verdict.

A Worked Comparison

Take Daniel's situation and write two competing explanations. Explanation A: the behavior is mainly connected with predictability, reduced decision load, transition support, or preference. Explanation B: the behavior is mainly connected with a rule that must be completed to prevent danger, guilt, contamination, or uncertainty. Now ask what each explanation predicts. If A is closer, accommodation or regulation may reduce distress without requiring the person to defeat a fear. If B is closer, reducing compulsive responding to feared uncertainty may be clinically relevant. If both predictions fit at different times, co-occurrence becomes a serious possibility.

This method prevents a common reasoning error: treating the name of an action as if it revealed its function. 'Checking,' 'repeating,' 'collecting,' 'researching,' and 'avoiding' are verbs, not diagnoses. A person can research a favorite topic for pleasure, research a feared disease for reassurance, or do both in the same evening. Ask what happened before, what the act was supposed to accomplish, and what happened after.

What Treatment Response Can Tell You

Treatment response is information, but it is not a home diagnostic test. ERP is an evidence-based component of CBT for OCD, and studies suggest adapted CBT can help autistic people who genuinely have co-occurring OCD (Russell et al., 2013; Flygare et al., 2020; National Institute for Health and Care Excellence [NICE], 2005/2019). That does not mean every repetitive autistic behavior should be targeted with exposure. If the target is sensory regulation, communication support, or a stable routine rather than an OCD compulsion, removing it can increase distress without treating the problem you meant to treat.

The safer principle is target accuracy. A clinician should identify the feared prediction or compulsive rule before asking you to resist a behavior as part of ERP. Adaptations may include clearer structure, concrete language, slower pacing, attention to sensory needs, and explicit differentiation between OCD goals and autism-related supports. If treatment repeatedly feels aimed at the wrong mechanism,

bring that observation back to the clinician rather than trying to push through on principle.

What Appearance Gets Wrong

A quick label can hide mixed functions. With repeated sequences, three mistakes are especially common. The first is assuming that visible anxiety proves OCD. A disrupted autistic routine or sensory overload can produce intense anxiety without a compulsion being present. The second is assuming that enjoyment rules OCD out. A person can feel temporary relief after a compulsion, and relief can be mistaken for preference. The third is assuming that a behavior has one function forever. A lifelong routine can later become entangled with OCD, or a person can begin using a familiar autistic behavior as part of a new threat-reduction rule.

For that reason, describe episodes rather than traits whenever you can. Instead of writing, "I always do this because I am autistic," record one recent example. Instead of writing, "This is definitely OCD," record the feared possibility, the rule, and what the behavior was supposed to prevent. Good differential assessment is built from patterns across examples. It is also allowed to end with more than one explanation.

Questions to Take to a Clinician

Bring examples instead of conclusions. Useful questions include: 'What makes you think this behavior is a compulsion rather than a regulating repetitive behavior?' 'What feared outcome or uncertainty are we targeting?' 'How are you accounting for sensory needs and developmental history?' 'Could both autism and OCD be present?' 'How will we know whether this intervention is reducing OCD rather than simply increasing my tolerance of distress from losing a useful support?'

A good assessment is not a debate you have to win. It is a process of making the evidence visible. You can help by naming the sequence precisely: what happened, what you thought or sensed, what you did, what you hoped the act would change, and what happened next. That gives a clinician something more useful than a checklist score alone.

Try the Four-Clue Overlap Map

Choose one example of repeated sequences. On one page, make four headings: Trigger, Function, Interruption, History. Under Trigger, record what came first. Under Function, record what the behavior was meant to change. Under Interruption, record the kind of distress that appears if you stop. Under History, record when the pattern first appeared and whether it has changed. Add a final line called 'What I am not sure about.' That last line is often the most useful one to bring to assessment.

In a Nutshell

The visible behavior is the beginning of the question, not the answer. For repeated sequences, look at trigger, function, interruption, and history before assigning meaning. Autism-related repetition can be valuable, regulating, pleasurable, or stabilizing. OCD compulsions are typically recruited into a cycle of threat, doubt, or rule-driven relief. Some experiences sit between those descriptions, and some people have both conditions. Your task is not to diagnose yourself from one clue. It is to build a clearer account of what is happening so the right professional questions can be asked.

References

National Institute of Mental Health. (n.d.-a). Autism spectrum disorder. https://www.nimh.nih.gov/health/publications/autism-spectrum-disorder

National Institute of Mental Health. (n.d.-b). Obsessive-compulsive disorder. https://www.nimh.nih.gov/health/topics/obsessive-compulsive-disorder-ocd

Cath, D. C., Ran, N., Smit, J. H., van Balkom, A. J. L. M., & Comijs, H. C. (2008). Symptom overlap between autism spectrum disorder, generalized social anxiety disorder and obsessive-compulsive disorder in adults: A preliminary case-controlled study. Psychopathology, 41(2), 101-110. https://pubmed.ncbi.nlm.nih.gov/18033980/

Santore, L. A., Gerber, A. H., Gioia, A. N., Bianchi, R., Talledo, F., Peris, T. S., & Lerner, M. D. (2020). Felt but not seen: Observed restricted repetitive behaviors are associated with self-report but not parent-report obsessive-compulsive disorder symptoms in youth with autism. Autism, 24(4), 983-994. https://pmc.ncbi.nlm.nih.gov/articles/PMC7337249/

Long, H. A., Rodgers, J., & South, M. (2024). 'Autism is the arena and OCD is the lion': Autistic adults' experiences of co-occurring obsessive-compulsive disorder. Autism. https://pmc.ncbi.nlm.nih.gov/articles/PMC11497754/

Wikramanayake, W. N. M., Mandy, W., Shahper, S., Kaur, S., Kolli, S., Osman, S., Reid, J., Jefferies-Sewell, K., & Fineberg, N. A. (2018). Autism spectrum disorders in adult outpatients with obsessive compulsive disorder in the UK. International Journal of Psychiatry in Clinical Practice, 22(1), 54-62. https://pubmed.ncbi.nlm.nih.gov/28705096/

Meier, S. M., Petersen, L., Schendel, D. E., Mattheisen, M., Mortensen, P. B., & Mors, O. (2015). Obsessive-compulsive disorder and autism spectrum disorders: Longitudinal and offspring risk. PLOS ONE, 10(11), e0141703. https://pubmed.ncbi.nlm.nih.gov/26558765/

Russell, A. J., Jassi, A., Fullana, M. A., Mack, H., Johnston, K., Heyman, I., Murphy, D. G., & Mataix-Cols, D. (2013). Cognitive behavior therapy for comorbid obsessive-compulsive disorder in high-functioning autism spectrum disorders: A randomized controlled trial.

Depression and Anxiety, 30(8), 697-708. https://pubmed.ncbi.nlm.nih.gov/23389964/

Flygare, O., Andersson, E., Ringberg, H., Hellstadius, K., Edbacken, J., Enander, J., Ljotsson, B., Mataix-Cols, D., & Serlachius, E. (2020). Adapted cognitive behavior therapy for obsessive-compulsive disorder with co-occurring autism spectrum disorder: A clinical effectiveness study. Autism, 24(1), 190-199. https://pubmed.ncbi.nlm.nih.gov/31187645/

National Institute for Health and Care Excellence. (2005, surveillance updated 2019). Obsessive-compulsive disorder and body dysmorphic disorder: Treatment (CG31). https://www.nice.org.uk/guidance/cg31

Chapter 5 Interests and Obsessions

Leila can spend an afternoon reading train timetables and feels restored. She also gets violent intrusive images that she finds repellent and spends hours reviewing whether they mean something about her. The outside view is simple: repetition. The inside story is not. A movement, question, sequence, or thought can be repeated for several reasons, and those reasons matter more than the photograph of the behavior. This chapter uses a composite scenario. Leila's details are blended from common patterns described in the literature and are not a portrait of one real person.

Autism and OCD can both include repetition. Autism is defined in part by restricted or repetitive patterns of behavior, interests, or activities, while OCD involves obsessions, compulsions, or both (National Institute of Mental Health [NIMH], n.d.-a; National Institute of Mental Health [NIMH], n.d.-b). That overlap is exactly why appearance is a poor shortcut. The useful question is not simply, 'Is it repetitive?' It is, 'What job is the repetition doing?'

The Chapter Principle

Use the Four-Clue Overlap Map: trigger, function, interruption, and history. For intense thought, an autism-related pattern may be connected with pleasure, curiosity, identity, expertise, and voluntary return. An OCD pattern is more likely when the act is recruited for intrusive unwanted content that provokes distress or a need to respond. None of these clues diagnoses anything by itself. Together they make a better clinical conversation.

Clue One Trigger

Start with what comes immediately before the behavior. A sensory demand, sudden transition, boredom, excitement, or need for focus can point toward regulation or predictability. A spike of doubt,

contamination fear, moral fear, harm image, or 'what if' question can point toward an OCD cycle. The same person can have both. The goal is to describe the sequence without deciding the label first.

Write the trigger as a camera could record it. 'The plan changed five minutes before we left' is better than 'I was triggered.' 'I noticed a thought that I might have left the stove on' is better than 'My anxiety got bad.' Concrete language lets a clinician ask the next question. Research comparing autism and OCD supports careful attention to phenomenology rather than assuming repetitive acts are equivalent (Cath et al., 2008; Santore et al., 2020).

Clue Two Function

Function means what the behavior is trying to change. Does it add useful sensation, organize attention, reduce overload, preserve a preferred pattern, or make an activity enjoyable? Those are different from trying to cancel danger, prove innocence, remove doubt, achieve a protective feeling, or satisfy a rule that says something bad will happen otherwise. In practice, mixed motives are common. You do not need a perfectly clean answer.

Ask a harder question: if there were no feared consequence at all, would you still want to do it? If the answer is yes because the act feels good, helps concentration, supports transition, or is part of a valued interest, that is information. If the answer is no, and the act feels like a tax paid to reduce threat or doubt, that is different information. Qualitative research with autistic adults who also have OCD describes how difficult and important this distinction can be (Long et al., 2024; Wikramanayake et al., 2018).

Clue Three Interruption

Interruption is not a morality test. Notice what kind of distress appears when the pattern is blocked. Sensory discomfort, disorganization, loss of focus, frustration at abrupt change, or a feeling of being

neurologically overloaded can occur around autistic routines and repetitive behavior. OCD interruption more often exposes the feared uncertainty the compulsion was managing: 'What if I did not check enough?' 'What if the contamination spreads?' 'What if this thought means I am dangerous?'

There is overlap here too. Autistic people can feel intense anxiety when a routine is interrupted, and people with OCD can describe bodily discomfort or a 'not just right' feeling rather than a clear catastrophic belief. That is why one clue never settles the question. The pattern across all four clues is more informative than any single answer.

Clue Four History

History asks when the pattern began and what else was true at the time. Autism is developmental, so a clinician assessing autism looks for a broader developmental pattern, not only current repetition. OCD can begin in childhood, adolescence, or adulthood and may wax and wane. A new ritual appearing after a period of intrusive doubt tells a different story from a lifelong preference for the same sensory input or sequence. Population and clinic studies show meaningful co-occurrence, so history should leave room for both rather than forcing an either-or answer (Meier et al., 2015; Wikramanayake et al., 2018).

If you can, collect examples from more than one age and setting. Old school reports, family recollections, childhood interests, early sensory patterns, and previous treatment responses can all be useful. Family memory is imperfect, and lack of documentation does not prove absence. Treat it as evidence to discuss, not a verdict.

A Worked Comparison

Take Leila's situation and write two competing explanations. Explanation A: the behavior is mainly connected with pleasure, curiosity, identity, expertise, and voluntary return. Explanation B: the behavior is mainly connected with intrusive unwanted content that provokes distress or a need to respond. Now ask what each explanation predicts. If A is closer, accommodation or regulation may reduce distress without requiring the person to defeat a fear. If B is closer, reducing compulsive responding to feared uncertainty may be clinically relevant. If both predictions fit at different times, co-occurrence becomes a serious possibility.

This method prevents a common reasoning error: treating the name of an action as if it revealed its function. 'Checking,' 'repeating,' 'collecting,' 'researching,' and 'avoiding' are verbs, not diagnoses. A person can research a favorite topic for pleasure, research a feared disease for reassurance, or do both in the same evening. Ask what happened before, what the act was supposed to accomplish, and what happened after.

What Treatment Response Can Tell You

Treatment response is information, but it is not a home diagnostic test. ERP is an evidence-based component of CBT for OCD, and studies suggest adapted CBT can help autistic people who genuinely have co-occurring OCD (Russell et al., 2013; Flygare et al., 2020; National Institute for Health and Care Excellence [NICE], 2005/2019). That does not mean every repetitive autistic behavior should be targeted with exposure. If the target is sensory regulation, communication support, or a stable routine rather than an OCD compulsion, removing it can increase distress without treating the problem you meant to treat.

The safer principle is target accuracy. A clinician should identify the feared prediction or compulsive rule before asking you to resist a behavior as part of ERP. Adaptations may include clearer structure, concrete language, slower pacing, attention to sensory needs, and explicit differentiation between OCD goals and autism-related supports. If treatment repeatedly feels aimed at the wrong mechanism, bring that observation back to the clinician rather than trying to push through on principle.

What Appearance Gets Wrong

A quick label can hide mixed functions. With intense thought, three mistakes are especially common. The first is assuming that visible anxiety proves OCD. A disrupted autistic routine or sensory overload can produce intense anxiety without a compulsion being present. The second is assuming that enjoyment rules OCD out. A person can feel temporary relief after a compulsion, and relief can be mistaken for preference. The third is assuming that a behavior has one function forever. A lifelong routine can later become entangled with OCD, or a person can begin using a familiar autistic behavior as part of a new threat-reduction rule.

For that reason, describe episodes rather than traits whenever you can. Instead of writing, "I always do this because I am autistic," record one recent example. Instead of writing, "This is definitely OCD," record the feared possibility, the rule, and what the behavior was supposed to prevent. Good differential assessment is built from patterns across examples. It is also allowed to end with more than one explanation.

Interest Has a Different Texture

A strong interest can occupy a great deal of time and still be wanted. The person returns because the subject is rewarding, organizing, aesthetically satisfying, socially meaningful, or connected with expertise. Time spent is therefore not enough to distinguish an interest from an obsession. Intensity is not enough either.

OCD obsessions are usually experienced as intrusive or unwanted, even when the topic is something the person genuinely cares about. The problem is often not the subject itself but the meaning attached to a thought: the demand to prove that a feared possibility is false, the sense that uncertainty is intolerable, or the belief that thinking something says something dangerous about character. That can lead to research, checking, reviewing, or reassurance that looks like deep interest from the outside.

Ask what happens after an hour with the topic. A valued interest may leave you energized, settled, informed, or happily absorbed. An OCD loop often leaves the original question hungry for another answer. That contrast is not universal, but it is useful evidence. The important distinction is not whether the topic is unusual or intense. It is whether engagement is mainly chosen and rewarding, mainly compelled by threat and doubt, or a mixture that changes from one episode to another.

Questions to Take to a Clinician

Bring examples instead of conclusions. Useful questions include: 'What makes you think this behavior is a compulsion rather than a regulating repetitive behavior?' 'What feared outcome or uncertainty are we targeting?' 'How are you accounting for sensory needs and developmental history?' 'Could both autism and OCD be present?' 'How will we know whether this intervention is reducing OCD rather than simply increasing my tolerance of distress from losing a useful support?'

A good assessment is not a debate you have to win. It is a process of making the evidence visible. You can help by naming the sequence precisely: what happened, what you thought or sensed, what you did, what you hoped the act would change, and what happened next. That gives a clinician something more useful than a checklist score alone.

Try the Four-Clue Overlap Map

Choose one example of intense thought. On one page, make four headings: Trigger, Function, Interruption, History. Under Trigger, record what came first. Under Function, record what the behavior was meant to change. Under Interruption, record the kind of distress that appears if you stop. Under History, record when the pattern first appeared and whether it has changed. Add a final line called 'What I am not sure about.' That last line is often the most useful one to bring to assessment.

Principles to Remember

The visible behavior is the beginning of the question, not the answer. For intense thought, look at trigger, function, interruption, and history before assigning meaning. Autism-related repetition can be valuable, regulating, pleasurable, or stabilizing. OCD compulsions are typically recruited into a cycle of threat, doubt, or rule-driven relief. Some experiences sit between those descriptions, and some people have both conditions. Your task is not to diagnose yourself from one clue. It is to build a clearer account of what is happening so the right professional questions can be asked.

References

National Institute of Mental Health. (n.d.-a). Autism spectrum disorder. https://www.nimh.nih.gov/health/publications/autism-spectrum-disorder

National Institute of Mental Health. (n.d.-b). Obsessive-compulsive disorder. https://www.nimh.nih.gov/health/topics/obsessive-compulsive-disorder-ocd

Cath, D. C., Ran, N., Smit, J. H., van Balkom, A. J. L. M., & Comijs, H. C. (2008). Symptom overlap between autism spectrum disorder, generalized social anxiety disorder and obsessive-compulsive disorder in adults: A preliminary case-controlled study. Psychopathology, 41(2), 101-110. https://pubmed.ncbi.nlm.nih.gov/18033980/

Santore, L. A., Gerber, A. H., Gioia, A. N., Bianchi, R., Talledo, F., Peris, T. S., & Lerner, M. D. (2020). Felt but not seen: Observed restricted repetitive behaviors are associated with self-report but not

parent-report obsessive-compulsive disorder symptoms in youth with autism. Autism, 24(4), 983-994. https://pmc.ncbi.nlm.nih.gov/articles/PMC7337249/

Long, H. A., Rodgers, J., & South, M. (2024). 'Autism is the arena and OCD is the lion': Autistic adults' experiences of co-occurring obsessive-compulsive disorder. Autism. https://pmc.ncbi.nlm.nih.gov/articles/PMC11497754/

Wikramanayake, W. N. M., Mandy, W., Shahper, S., Kaur, S., Kolli, S., Osman, S., Reid, J., Jefferies-Sewell, K., & Fineberg, N. A. (2018). Autism spectrum disorders in adult outpatients with obsessive compulsive disorder in the UK. International Journal of Psychiatry in Clinical Practice, 22(1), 54-62. https://pubmed.ncbi.nlm.nih.gov/28705096/

Meier, S. M., Petersen, L., Schendel, D. E., Mattheisen, M., Mortensen, P. B., & Mors, O. (2015). Obsessive-compulsive disorder and autism spectrum disorders: Longitudinal and offspring risk. PLOS ONE, 10(11), e0141703. https://pubmed.ncbi.nlm.nih.gov/26558765/

Russell, A. J., Jassi, A., Fullana, M. A., Mack, H., Johnston, K., Heyman, I., Murphy, D. G., & Mataix-Cols, D. (2013). Cognitive behavior therapy for comorbid obsessive-compulsive disorder in high-functioning autism spectrum disorders: A randomized controlled trial. Depression and Anxiety, 30(8), 697-708. https://pubmed.ncbi.nlm.nih.gov/23389964/

Flygare, O., Andersson, E., Ringberg, H., Hellstadius, K., Edbacken, J., Enander, J., Ljotsson, B., Mataix-Cols, D., & Serlachius, E. (2020). Adapted cognitive behavior therapy for obsessive-compulsive disorder with co-occurring autism spectrum disorder: A clinical effectiveness study. Autism, 24(1), 190-199. https://pubmed.ncbi.nlm.nih.gov/31187645/

National Institute for Health and Care Excellence. (2005, surveillance updated 2019). Obsessive-compulsive disorder and body dysmorphic disorder: Treatment (CG31). https://www.nice.org.uk/guidance/cg31

Chapter 6 Sameness and Certainty

Predictability and certainty can look alike from a distance, but they solve different problems. Marcus wants the same desk at work because the lighting and traffic pattern are tolerable there. He also rereads an email until he feels certain he did not accidentally insult anyone. The outside view is simple: repetition. The inside story is not. A movement, question, sequence, or thought can be repeated for several reasons, and those reasons matter more than the photograph of the behavior. This chapter uses a composite scenario. Marcus's details are blended from common patterns described in the literature and are not a portrait of one real person.

Autism and OCD can both include repetition. Autism is defined in part by restricted or repetitive patterns of behavior, interests, or activities, while OCD involves obsessions, compulsions, or both (National Institute of Mental Health [NIMH], n.d.-a; National Institute of Mental Health [NIMH], n.d.-b). That overlap is exactly why appearance is a poor shortcut. The useful question is not simply, 'Is it repetitive?' It is, 'What job is the repetition doing?'

The Chapter Principle

Use the Four-Clue Overlap Map: trigger, function, interruption, and history. For resistance to change, an autism-related pattern may be connected with predictability, reduced sensory or cognitive load, and continuity. An OCD pattern is more likely when the act is recruited for the impossible demand for complete certainty before moving on. None of these clues diagnoses anything by itself. Together they make a better clinical conversation.

Clue One Trigger

Start with what comes immediately before the behavior. A sensory demand, sudden transition, boredom, excitement, or need for focus can

point toward regulation or predictability. A spike of doubt, contamination fear, moral fear, harm image, or 'what if' question can point toward an OCD cycle. The same person can have both. The goal is to describe the sequence without deciding the label first.

Write the trigger as a camera could record it. 'The plan changed five minutes before we left' is better than 'I was triggered.' 'I noticed a thought that I might have left the stove on' is better than 'My anxiety got bad.' Concrete language lets a clinician ask the next question. Research comparing autism and OCD supports careful attention to phenomenology rather than assuming repetitive acts are equivalent (Cath et al., 2008; Santore et al., 2020).

Clue Two Function

Function means what the behavior is trying to change. Does it add useful sensation, organize attention, reduce overload, preserve a preferred pattern, or make an activity enjoyable? Those are different from trying to cancel danger, prove innocence, remove doubt, achieve a protective feeling, or satisfy a rule that says something bad will happen otherwise. In practice, mixed motives are common. You do not need a perfectly clean answer.

Ask a harder question: if there were no feared consequence at all, would you still want to do it? If the answer is yes because the act feels good, helps concentration, supports transition, or is part of a valued interest, that is information. If the answer is no, and the act feels like a tax paid to reduce threat or doubt, that is different information. Qualitative research with autistic adults who also have OCD describes how difficult and important this distinction can be (Long et al., 2024; Wikramanayake et al., 2018).

Clue Three Interruption

Interruption is not a morality test. Notice what kind of distress appears when the pattern is blocked. Sensory discomfort, disorganization, loss

of focus, frustration at abrupt change, or a feeling of being neurologically overloaded can occur around autistic routines and repetitive behavior. OCD interruption more often exposes the feared uncertainty the compulsion was managing: 'What if I did not check enough?' 'What if the contamination spreads?' 'What if this thought means I am dangerous?'

There is overlap here too. Autistic people can feel intense anxiety when a routine is interrupted, and people with OCD can describe bodily discomfort or a 'not just right' feeling rather than a clear catastrophic belief. That is why one clue never settles the question. The pattern across all four clues is more informative than any single answer.

Clue Four History

History asks when the pattern began and what else was true at the time. Autism is developmental, so a clinician assessing autism looks for a broader developmental pattern, not only current repetition. OCD can begin in childhood, adolescence, or adulthood and may wax and wane. A new ritual appearing after a period of intrusive doubt tells a different story from a lifelong preference for the same sensory input or sequence. Population and clinic studies show meaningful co-occurrence, so history should leave room for both rather than forcing an either-or answer (Meier et al., 2015; Wikramanayake et al., 2018).

If you can, collect examples from more than one age and setting. Old school reports, family recollections, childhood interests, early sensory patterns, and previous treatment responses can all be useful. Family memory is imperfect, and lack of documentation does not prove absence. Treat it as evidence to discuss, not a verdict.

A Worked Comparison

Take Marcus's situation and write two competing explanations. Explanation A: the behavior is mainly connected with predictability, reduced sensory or cognitive load, and continuity. Explanation B: the behavior is mainly connected with the impossible demand for complete certainty before moving on. Now ask what each explanation predicts. If A is closer, accommodation or regulation may reduce distress without requiring the person to defeat a fear. If B is closer, reducing compulsive responding to feared uncertainty may be clinically relevant. If both predictions fit at different times, co-occurrence becomes a serious possibility.

This method prevents a common reasoning error: treating the name of an action as if it revealed its function. 'Checking,' 'repeating,' 'collecting,' 'researching,' and 'avoiding' are verbs, not diagnoses. A person can research a favorite topic for pleasure, research a feared disease for reassurance, or do both in the same evening. Ask what happened before, what the act was supposed to accomplish, and what happened after.

What Treatment Response Can Tell You

Treatment response is information, but it is not a home diagnostic test. ERP is an evidence-based component of CBT for OCD, and studies suggest adapted CBT can help autistic people who genuinely have co-occurring OCD (Russell et al., 2013; Flygare et al., 2020; National Institute for Health and Care Excellence [NICE], 2005/2019). That does not mean every repetitive autistic behavior should be targeted with exposure. If the target is sensory regulation, communication support, or a stable routine rather than an OCD compulsion, removing it can increase distress without treating the problem you meant to treat.

The safer principle is target accuracy. A clinician should identify the feared prediction or compulsive rule before asking you to resist a behavior as part of ERP. Adaptations may include clearer structure, concrete language, slower pacing, attention to sensory needs, and explicit differentiation between OCD goals and autism-related supports. If treatment repeatedly feels aimed at the wrong mechanism,

bring that observation back to the clinician rather than trying to push through on principle.

What Appearance Gets Wrong

A quick label can hide mixed functions. With resistance to change, three mistakes are especially common. The first is assuming that visible anxiety proves OCD. A disrupted autistic routine or sensory overload can produce intense anxiety without a compulsion being present. The second is assuming that enjoyment rules OCD out. A person can feel temporary relief after a compulsion, and relief can be mistaken for preference. The third is assuming that a behavior has one function forever. A lifelong routine can later become entangled with OCD, or a person can begin using a familiar autistic behavior as part of a new threat-reduction rule.

For that reason, describe episodes rather than traits whenever you can. Instead of writing, "I always do this because I am autistic," record one recent example. Instead of writing, "This is definitely OCD," record the feared possibility, the rule, and what the behavior was supposed to prevent. Good differential assessment is built from patterns across examples. It is also allowed to end with more than one explanation.

Questions to Take to a Clinician

Bring examples instead of conclusions. Useful questions include: 'What makes you think this behavior is a compulsion rather than a regulating repetitive behavior?' 'What feared outcome or uncertainty are we targeting?' 'How are you accounting for sensory needs and developmental history?' 'Could both autism and OCD be present?' 'How will we know whether this intervention is reducing OCD rather than simply increasing my tolerance of distress from losing a useful support?'

A good assessment is not a debate you have to win. It is a process of making the evidence visible. You can help by naming the sequence precisely: what happened, what you thought or sensed, what you did, what you hoped the act would change, and what happened next. That gives a clinician something more useful than a checklist score alone.

Try the Four-Clue Overlap Map

Choose one example of resistance to change. On one page, make four headings: Trigger, Function, Interruption, History. Under Trigger, record what came first. Under Function, record what the behavior was meant to change. Under Interruption, record the kind of distress that appears if you stop. Under History, record when the pattern first appeared and whether it has changed. Add a final line called 'What I am not sure about.' That last line is often the most useful one to bring to assessment.

In a Nutshell

The visible behavior is the beginning of the question, not the answer. For resistance to change, look at trigger, function, interruption, and history before assigning meaning. Autism-related repetition can be valuable, regulating, pleasurable, or stabilizing. OCD compulsions are typically recruited into a cycle of threat, doubt, or rule-driven relief. Some experiences sit between those descriptions, and some people have both conditions. Your task is not to diagnose yourself from one clue. It is to build a clearer account of what is happening so the right professional questions can be asked.

References

National Institute of Mental Health. (n.d.-a). Autism spectrum disorder. https://www.nimh.nih.gov/health/publications/autism-spectrum-disorder

National Institute of Mental Health. (n.d.-b). Obsessive-compulsive disorder. https://www.nimh.nih.gov/health/topics/obsessive-compulsive-disorder-ocd

Cath, D. C., Ran, N., Smit, J. H., van Balkom, A. J. L. M., & Comijs, H. C. (2008). Symptom overlap between autism spectrum disorder, generalized social anxiety disorder and obsessive-compulsive disorder in adults: A preliminary case-controlled study. Psychopathology, 41(2), 101-110. https://pubmed.ncbi.nlm.nih.gov/18033980/

Santore, L. A., Gerber, A. H., Gioia, A. N., Bianchi, R., Talledo, F., Peris, T. S., & Lerner, M. D. (2020). Felt but not seen: Observed restricted repetitive behaviors are associated with self-report but not parent-report obsessive-compulsive disorder symptoms in youth with autism. Autism, 24(4), 983-994. https://pmc.ncbi.nlm.nih.gov/articles/PMC7337249/

Long, H. A., Rodgers, J., & South, M. (2024). 'Autism is the arena and OCD is the lion': Autistic adults' experiences of co-occurring obsessive-compulsive disorder. Autism. https://pmc.ncbi.nlm.nih.gov/articles/PMC11497754/

Wikramanayake, W. N. M., Mandy, W., Shahper, S., Kaur, S., Kolli, S., Osman, S., Reid, J., Jefferies-Sewell, K., & Fineberg, N. A. (2018). Autism spectrum disorders in adult outpatients with obsessive compulsive disorder in the UK. International Journal of Psychiatry in Clinical Practice, 22(1), 54-62. https://pubmed.ncbi.nlm.nih.gov/28705096/

Meier, S. M., Petersen, L., Schendel, D. E., Mattheisen, M., Mortensen, P. B., & Mors, O. (2015). Obsessive-compulsive disorder and autism spectrum disorders: Longitudinal and offspring risk. PLOS ONE, 10(11), e0141703. https://pubmed.ncbi.nlm.nih.gov/26558765/

Russell, A. J., Jassi, A., Fullana, M. A., Mack, H., Johnston, K., Heyman, I., Murphy, D. G., & Mataix-Cols, D. (2013). Cognitive behavior therapy for comorbid obsessive-compulsive disorder in high-functioning autism spectrum disorders: A randomized controlled trial.

Depression and Anxiety, 30(8), 697-708. https://pubmed.ncbi.nlm.nih.gov/23389964/

Flygare, O., Andersson, E., Ringberg, H., Hellstadius, K., Edbacken, J., Enander, J., Ljotsson, B., Mataix-Cols, D., & Serlachius, E. (2020). Adapted cognitive behavior therapy for obsessive-compulsive disorder with co-occurring autism spectrum disorder: A clinical effectiveness study. Autism, 24(1), 190-199. https://pubmed.ncbi.nlm.nih.gov/31187645/

National Institute for Health and Care Excellence. (2005, surveillance updated 2019). Obsessive-compulsive disorder and body dysmorphic disorder: Treatment (CG31). https://www.nice.org.uk/guidance/cg31

Chapter 7 Sensory Distress and Fear

Sofia avoids a grocery aisle because the refrigeration hum is physically punishing. She avoids a different aisle because she fears a contaminant and later washes her hands according to a rigid rule. The outside view is simple: repetition. The inside story is not. A movement, question, sequence, or thought can be repeated for several reasons, and those reasons matter more than the photograph of the behavior. This chapter uses a composite scenario. Sofia's details are blended from common patterns described in the literature and are not a portrait of one real person.

Autism and OCD can both include repetition. Autism is defined in part by restricted or repetitive patterns of behavior, interests, or activities, while OCD involves obsessions, compulsions, or both (National Institute of Mental Health [NIMH], n.d.-a; National Institute of Mental Health [NIMH], n.d.-b). That overlap is exactly why appearance is a poor shortcut. The useful question is not simply, 'Is it repetitive?' It is, 'What job is the repetition doing?'

The Chapter Principle

Use the Four-Clue Overlap Map: trigger, function, interruption, and history. For avoidance, an autism-related pattern may be connected with protecting against overwhelming sensory input or overload. An OCD pattern is more likely when the act is recruited for escaping a feared consequence or preventing anxiety from rising. None of these clues diagnoses anything by itself. Together they make a better clinical conversation.

Clue One Trigger

Start with what comes immediately before the behavior. A sensory demand, sudden transition, boredom, excitement, or need for focus can point toward regulation or predictability. A spike of doubt,

contamination fear, moral fear, harm image, or 'what if' question can point toward an OCD cycle. The same person can have both. The goal is to describe the sequence without deciding the label first.

Write the trigger as a camera could record it. 'The plan changed five minutes before we left' is better than 'I was triggered.' 'I noticed a thought that I might have left the stove on' is better than 'My anxiety got bad.' Concrete language lets a clinician ask the next question. Research comparing autism and OCD supports careful attention to phenomenology rather than assuming repetitive acts are equivalent (Cath et al., 2008; Santore et al., 2020).

Clue Two Function

Function means what the behavior is trying to change. Does it add useful sensation, organize attention, reduce overload, preserve a preferred pattern, or make an activity enjoyable? Those are different from trying to cancel danger, prove innocence, remove doubt, achieve a protective feeling, or satisfy a rule that says something bad will happen otherwise. In practice, mixed motives are common. You do not need a perfectly clean answer.

Ask a harder question: if there were no feared consequence at all, would you still want to do it? If the answer is yes because the act feels good, helps concentration, supports transition, or is part of a valued interest, that is information. If the answer is no, and the act feels like a tax paid to reduce threat or doubt, that is different information. Qualitative research with autistic adults who also have OCD describes how difficult and important this distinction can be (Long et al., 2024; Wikramanayake et al., 2018).

Clue Three Interruption

Interruption is not a morality test. Notice what kind of distress appears when the pattern is blocked. Sensory discomfort, disorganization, loss of focus, frustration at abrupt change, or a feeling of being

neurologically overloaded can occur around autistic routines and repetitive behavior. OCD interruption more often exposes the feared uncertainty the compulsion was managing: 'What if I did not check enough?' 'What if the contamination spreads?' 'What if this thought means I am dangerous?'

There is overlap here too. Autistic people can feel intense anxiety when a routine is interrupted, and people with OCD can describe bodily discomfort or a 'not just right' feeling rather than a clear catastrophic belief. That is why one clue never settles the question. The pattern across all four clues is more informative than any single answer.

Clue Four History

History asks when the pattern began and what else was true at the time. Autism is developmental, so a clinician assessing autism looks for a broader developmental pattern, not only current repetition. OCD can begin in childhood, adolescence, or adulthood and may wax and wane. A new ritual appearing after a period of intrusive doubt tells a different story from a lifelong preference for the same sensory input or sequence. Population and clinic studies show meaningful co-occurrence, so history should leave room for both rather than forcing an either-or answer (Meier et al., 2015; Wikramanayake et al., 2018).

If you can, collect examples from more than one age and setting. Old school reports, family recollections, childhood interests, early sensory patterns, and previous treatment responses can all be useful. Family memory is imperfect, and lack of documentation does not prove absence. Treat it as evidence to discuss, not a verdict.

A Worked Comparison

Take Sofia's situation and write two competing explanations. Explanation A: the behavior is mainly connected with protecting against overwhelming sensory input or overload. Explanation B: the behavior is mainly connected with escaping a feared consequence or preventing anxiety from rising. Now ask what each explanation predicts. If A is closer, accommodation or regulation may reduce distress without requiring the person to defeat a fear. If B is closer, reducing compulsive responding to feared uncertainty may be clinically relevant. If both predictions fit at different times, co-occurrence becomes a serious possibility.

This method prevents a common reasoning error: treating the name of an action as if it revealed its function. 'Checking,' 'repeating,' 'collecting,' 'researching,' and 'avoiding' are verbs, not diagnoses. A person can research a favorite topic for pleasure, research a feared disease for reassurance, or do both in the same evening. Ask what happened before, what the act was supposed to accomplish, and what happened after.

What Treatment Response Can Tell You

Treatment response is information, but it is not a home diagnostic test. ERP is an evidence-based component of CBT for OCD, and studies suggest adapted CBT can help autistic people who genuinely have co-occurring OCD (Russell et al., 2013; Flygare et al., 2020; National Institute for Health and Care Excellence [NICE], 2005/2019). That does not mean every repetitive autistic behavior should be targeted with exposure. If the target is sensory regulation, communication support, or a stable routine rather than an OCD compulsion, removing it can increase distress without treating the problem you meant to treat.

The safer principle is target accuracy. A clinician should identify the feared prediction or compulsive rule before asking you to resist a behavior as part of ERP. Adaptations may include clearer structure, concrete language, slower pacing, attention to sensory needs, and explicit differentiation between OCD goals and autism-related supports. If treatment repeatedly feels aimed at the wrong mechanism, bring that observation back to the clinician rather than trying to push through on principle.

What Appearance Gets Wrong

A quick label can hide mixed functions. With avoidance, three mistakes are especially common. The first is assuming that visible anxiety proves OCD. A disrupted autistic routine or sensory overload can produce intense anxiety without a compulsion being present. The second is assuming that enjoyment rules OCD out. A person can feel temporary relief after a compulsion, and relief can be mistaken for preference. The third is assuming that a behavior has one function forever. A lifelong routine can later become entangled with OCD, or a person can begin using a familiar autistic behavior as part of a new threat-reduction rule.

For that reason, describe episodes rather than traits whenever you can. Instead of writing, "I always do this because I am autistic," record one recent example. Instead of writing, "This is definitely OCD," record the feared possibility, the rule, and what the behavior was supposed to prevent. Good differential assessment is built from patterns across examples. It is also allowed to end with more than one explanation.

Sensory Avoidance Needs Its Own Question

Sensory distress is concrete. A fluorescent light can hurt, a fabric can feel unbearable, a refrigeration motor can dominate attention, and a smell can make a space impossible to use. Avoiding those inputs may be a reasonable way to reduce overload. An exposure plan designed for a feared catastrophe is not automatically the right tool for a sensory threshold.

Fear avoidance has a different logic. The person may avoid a surface because touching it is linked to a contamination prediction, avoid driving because of a fear of causing harm, or avoid a word because saying it feels dangerous. The physical setting may be identical, but the feared consequence is doing the work.

Mixed cases are common. A public restroom can be genuinely difficult because of smell, noise, lighting, and unpredictability while also becoming the center of contamination compulsions. An assessor who asks only, "Do you avoid public restrooms?" has not yet separated the mechanisms. A better follow-up is, "What specifically are you trying to get away from?" If the answer includes both sensory pain and a feared contamination chain, both deserve attention. Removing the sensory burden may make OCD work more possible, while OCD treatment should still target the compulsive fear cycle rather than the sensory experience itself.

Questions to Take to a Clinician

Bring examples instead of conclusions. Useful questions include: 'What makes you think this behavior is a compulsion rather than a regulating repetitive behavior?' 'What feared outcome or uncertainty are we targeting?' 'How are you accounting for sensory needs and developmental history?' 'Could both autism and OCD be present?' 'How will we know whether this intervention is reducing OCD rather than simply increasing my tolerance of distress from losing a useful support?'

A good assessment is not a debate you have to win. It is a process of making the evidence visible. You can help by naming the sequence precisely: what happened, what you thought or sensed, what you did, what you hoped the act would change, and what happened next. That gives a clinician something more useful than a checklist score alone.

Try the Four-Clue Overlap Map

Choose one example of avoidance. On one page, make four headings: Trigger, Function, Interruption, History. Under Trigger, record what came first. Under Function, record what the behavior was meant to change. Under Interruption, record the kind of distress that appears if you stop. Under History, record when the pattern first appeared and whether it has changed. Add a final line called 'What I am not sure about.' That last line is often the most useful one to bring to assessment.

Principles to Remember

The visible behavior is the beginning of the question, not the answer. For avoidance, look at trigger, function, interruption, and history before assigning meaning. Autism-related repetition can be valuable, regulating, pleasurable, or stabilizing. OCD compulsions are typically recruited into a cycle of threat, doubt, or rule-driven relief. Some experiences sit between those descriptions, and some people have both conditions. Your task is not to diagnose yourself from one clue. It is to build a clearer account of what is happening so the right professional questions can be asked.

References

National Institute of Mental Health. (n.d.-a). Autism spectrum disorder. https://www.nimh.nih.gov/health/publications/autism-spectrum-disorder

National Institute of Mental Health. (n.d.-b). Obsessive-compulsive disorder. https://www.nimh.nih.gov/health/topics/obsessive-compulsive-disorder-ocd

Cath, D. C., Ran, N., Smit, J. H., van Balkom, A. J. L. M., & Comijs, H. C. (2008). Symptom overlap between autism spectrum disorder, generalized social anxiety disorder and obsessive-compulsive disorder in adults: A preliminary case-controlled study. Psychopathology, 41(2), 101-110. https://pubmed.ncbi.nlm.nih.gov/18033980/

Santore, L. A., Gerber, A. H., Gioia, A. N., Bianchi, R., Talledo, F., Peris, T. S., & Lerner, M. D. (2020). Felt but not seen: Observed restricted repetitive behaviors are associated with self-report but not

parent-report obsessive-compulsive disorder symptoms in youth with autism. Autism, 24(4), 983-994. https://pmc.ncbi.nlm.nih.gov/articles/PMC7337249/

Long, H. A., Rodgers, J., & South, M. (2024). 'Autism is the arena and OCD is the lion': Autistic adults' experiences of co-occurring obsessive-compulsive disorder. Autism. https://pmc.ncbi.nlm.nih.gov/articles/PMC11497754/

Wikramanayake, W. N. M., Mandy, W., Shahper, S., Kaur, S., Kolli, S., Osman, S., Reid, J., Jefferies-Sewell, K., & Fineberg, N. A. (2018). Autism spectrum disorders in adult outpatients with obsessive compulsive disorder in the UK. International Journal of Psychiatry in Clinical Practice, 22(1), 54-62. https://pubmed.ncbi.nlm.nih.gov/28705096/

Meier, S. M., Petersen, L., Schendel, D. E., Mattheisen, M., Mortensen, P. B., & Mors, O. (2015). Obsessive-compulsive disorder and autism spectrum disorders: Longitudinal and offspring risk. PLOS ONE, 10(11), e0141703. https://pubmed.ncbi.nlm.nih.gov/26558765/

Russell, A. J., Jassi, A., Fullana, M. A., Mack, H., Johnston, K., Heyman, I., Murphy, D. G., & Mataix-Cols, D. (2013). Cognitive behavior therapy for comorbid obsessive-compulsive disorder in high-functioning autism spectrum disorders: A randomized controlled trial. Depression and Anxiety, 30(8), 697-708. https://pubmed.ncbi.nlm.nih.gov/23389964/

Flygare, O., Andersson, E., Ringberg, H., Hellstadius, K., Edbacken, J., Enander, J., Ljotsson, B., Mataix-Cols, D., & Serlachius, E. (2020). Adapted cognitive behavior therapy for obsessive-compulsive disorder with co-occurring autism spectrum disorder: A clinical effectiveness study. Autism, 24(1), 190-199. https://pubmed.ncbi.nlm.nih.gov/31187645/

National Institute for Health and Care Excellence. (2005, surveillance updated 2019). Obsessive-compulsive disorder and body dysmorphic disorder: Treatment (CG31). https://www.nice.org.uk/guidance/cg31

Chapter 8 Intrusive Thoughts and Meaning

A thought can repeat without becoming an OCD obsession. Ethan notices a phrase looping in his head after hearing it once. The loop is irritating. A separate thought, that he might have harmed someone, pulls him into hours of checking. The outside view is simple: repetition. The inside story is not. A movement, question, sequence, or thought can be repeated for several reasons, and those reasons matter more than the photograph of the behavior. This chapter uses a composite scenario. Ethan's details are blended from common patterns described in the literature and are not a portrait of one real person.

Autism and OCD can both include repetition. Autism is defined in part by restricted or repetitive patterns of behavior, interests, or activities, while OCD involves obsessions, compulsions, or both (National Institute of Mental Health [NIMH], n.d.-a; National Institute of Mental Health [NIMH], n.d.-b). That overlap is exactly why appearance is a poor shortcut. The useful question is not simply, 'Is it repetitive?' It is, 'What job is the repetition doing?'

The Chapter Principle

Use the Four-Clue Overlap Map: trigger, function, interruption, and history. For unwanted mental events, an autism-related pattern may be connected with an autistic mind can have sticky, vivid, repetitive thoughts without those thoughts automatically being obsessions. An OCD pattern is more likely when the act is recruited for OCD often gives intrusive thoughts inflated meaning and recruits rituals, reassurance, or avoidance. None of these clues diagnoses anything by itself. Together they make a better clinical conversation.

Clue One Trigger

Start with what comes immediately before the behavior. A sensory demand, sudden transition, boredom, excitement, or need for focus can

point toward regulation or predictability. A spike of doubt, contamination fear, moral fear, harm image, or 'what if' question can point toward an OCD cycle. The same person can have both. The goal is to describe the sequence without deciding the label first.

Write the trigger as a camera could record it. 'The plan changed five minutes before we left' is better than 'I was triggered.' 'I noticed a thought that I might have left the stove on' is better than 'My anxiety got bad.' Concrete language lets a clinician ask the next question. Research comparing autism and OCD supports careful attention to phenomenology rather than assuming repetitive acts are equivalent (Cath et al., 2008; Santore et al., 2020).

Clue Two Function

Function means what the behavior is trying to change. Does it add useful sensation, organize attention, reduce overload, preserve a preferred pattern, or make an activity enjoyable? Those are different from trying to cancel danger, prove innocence, remove doubt, achieve a protective feeling, or satisfy a rule that says something bad will happen otherwise. In practice, mixed motives are common. You do not need a perfectly clean answer.

Ask a harder question: if there were no feared consequence at all, would you still want to do it? If the answer is yes because the act feels good, helps concentration, supports transition, or is part of a valued interest, that is information. If the answer is no, and the act feels like a tax paid to reduce threat or doubt, that is different information. Qualitative research with autistic adults who also have OCD describes how difficult and important this distinction can be (Long et al., 2024; Wikramanayake et al., 2018).

Clue Three Interruption

Interruption is not a morality test. Notice what kind of distress appears when the pattern is blocked. Sensory discomfort, disorganization, loss

of focus, frustration at abrupt change, or a feeling of being neurologically overloaded can occur around autistic routines and repetitive behavior. OCD interruption more often exposes the feared uncertainty the compulsion was managing: 'What if I did not check enough?' 'What if the contamination spreads?' 'What if this thought means I am dangerous?'

There is overlap here too. Autistic people can feel intense anxiety when a routine is interrupted, and people with OCD can describe bodily discomfort or a 'not just right' feeling rather than a clear catastrophic belief. That is why one clue never settles the question. The pattern across all four clues is more informative than any single answer.

Clue Four History

History asks when the pattern began and what else was true at the time. Autism is developmental, so a clinician assessing autism looks for a broader developmental pattern, not only current repetition. OCD can begin in childhood, adolescence, or adulthood and may wax and wane. A new ritual appearing after a period of intrusive doubt tells a different story from a lifelong preference for the same sensory input or sequence. Population and clinic studies show meaningful co-occurrence, so history should leave room for both rather than forcing an either-or answer (Meier et al., 2015; Wikramanayake et al., 2018).

If you can, collect examples from more than one age and setting. Old school reports, family recollections, childhood interests, early sensory patterns, and previous treatment responses can all be useful. Family memory is imperfect, and lack of documentation does not prove absence. Treat it as evidence to discuss, not a verdict.

A Worked Comparison

Take Ethan's situation and write two competing explanations. Explanation A: the behavior is mainly connected with an autistic mind can have sticky, vivid, repetitive thoughts without those thoughts automatically being obsessions. Explanation B: the behavior is mainly connected with OCD often gives intrusive thoughts inflated meaning and recruits rituals, reassurance, or avoidance. Now ask what each explanation predicts. If A is closer, accommodation or regulation may reduce distress without requiring the person to defeat a fear. If B is closer, reducing compulsive responding to feared uncertainty may be clinically relevant. If both predictions fit at different times, co-occurrence becomes a serious possibility.

This method prevents a common reasoning error: treating the name of an action as if it revealed its function. 'Checking,' 'repeating,' 'collecting,' 'researching,' and 'avoiding' are verbs, not diagnoses. A person can research a favorite topic for pleasure, research a feared disease for reassurance, or do both in the same evening. Ask what happened before, what the act was supposed to accomplish, and what happened after.

What Treatment Response Can Tell You

Treatment response is information, but it is not a home diagnostic test. ERP is an evidence-based component of CBT for OCD, and studies suggest adapted CBT can help autistic people who genuinely have co-occurring OCD (Russell et al., 2013; Flygare et al., 2020; National Institute for Health and Care Excellence [NICE], 2005/2019). That does not mean every repetitive autistic behavior should be targeted with exposure. If the target is sensory regulation, communication support, or a stable routine rather than an OCD compulsion, removing it can increase distress without treating the problem you meant to treat.

The safer principle is target accuracy. A clinician should identify the feared prediction or compulsive rule before asking you to resist a behavior as part of ERP. Adaptations may include clearer structure, concrete language, slower pacing, attention to sensory needs, and explicit differentiation between OCD goals and autism-related supports. If treatment repeatedly feels aimed at the wrong mechanism,

bring that observation back to the clinician rather than trying to push through on principle.

What Appearance Gets Wrong

A quick label can hide mixed functions. With unwanted mental events, three mistakes are especially common. The first is assuming that visible anxiety proves OCD. A disrupted autistic routine or sensory overload can produce intense anxiety without a compulsion being present. The second is assuming that enjoyment rules OCD out. A person can feel temporary relief after a compulsion, and relief can be mistaken for preference. The third is assuming that a behavior has one function forever. A lifelong routine can later become entangled with OCD, or a person can begin using a familiar autistic behavior as part of a new threat-reduction rule.

For that reason, describe episodes rather than traits whenever you can. Instead of writing, "I always do this because I am autistic," record one recent example. Instead of writing, "This is definitely OCD," record the feared possibility, the rule, and what the behavior was supposed to prevent. Good differential assessment is built from patterns across examples. It is also allowed to end with more than one explanation.

Questions to Take to a Clinician

Bring examples instead of conclusions. Useful questions include: 'What makes you think this behavior is a compulsion rather than a regulating repetitive behavior?' 'What feared outcome or uncertainty are we targeting?' 'How are you accounting for sensory needs and developmental history?' 'Could both autism and OCD be present?' 'How will we know whether this intervention is reducing OCD rather than simply increasing my tolerance of distress from losing a useful support?'

A good assessment is not a debate you have to win. It is a process of making the evidence visible. You can help by naming the sequence precisely: what happened, what you thought or sensed, what you did, what you hoped the act would change, and what happened next. That gives a clinician something more useful than a checklist score alone.

Try the Four-Clue Overlap Map

Choose one example of unwanted mental events. On one page, make four headings: Trigger, Function, Interruption, History. Under Trigger, record what came first. Under Function, record what the behavior was meant to change. Under Interruption, record the kind of distress that appears if you stop. Under History, record when the pattern first appeared and whether it has changed. Add a final line called 'What I am not sure about.' That last line is often the most useful one to bring to assessment.

In a Nutshell

The visible behavior is the beginning of the question, not the answer. For unwanted mental events, look at trigger, function, interruption, and history before assigning meaning. Autism-related repetition can be valuable, regulating, pleasurable, or stabilizing. OCD compulsions are typically recruited into a cycle of threat, doubt, or rule-driven relief. Some experiences sit between those descriptions, and some people have both conditions. Your task is not to diagnose yourself from one clue. It is to build a clearer account of what is happening so the right professional questions can be asked.

References

National Institute of Mental Health. (n.d.-a). Autism spectrum disorder. https://www.nimh.nih.gov/health/publications/autism-spectrum-disorder

National Institute of Mental Health. (n.d.-b). Obsessive-compulsive disorder. https://www.nimh.nih.gov/health/topics/obsessive-compulsive-disorder-ocd

Cath, D. C., Ran, N., Smit, J. H., van Balkom, A. J. L. M., & Comijs, H. C. (2008). Symptom overlap between autism spectrum disorder, generalized social anxiety disorder and obsessive-compulsive disorder in adults: A preliminary case-controlled study. Psychopathology, 41(2), 101-110. https://pubmed.ncbi.nlm.nih.gov/18033980/

Santore, L. A., Gerber, A. H., Gioia, A. N., Bianchi, R., Talledo, F., Peris, T. S., & Lerner, M. D. (2020). Felt but not seen: Observed restricted repetitive behaviors are associated with self-report but not parent-report obsessive-compulsive disorder symptoms in youth with autism. Autism, 24(4), 983-994. https://pmc.ncbi.nlm.nih.gov/articles/PMC7337249/

Long, H. A., Rodgers, J., & South, M. (2024). 'Autism is the arena and OCD is the lion': Autistic adults' experiences of co-occurring obsessive-compulsive disorder. Autism. https://pmc.ncbi.nlm.nih.gov/articles/PMC11497754/

Wikramanayake, W. N. M., Mandy, W., Shahper, S., Kaur, S., Kolli, S., Osman, S., Reid, J., Jefferies-Sewell, K., & Fineberg, N. A. (2018). Autism spectrum disorders in adult outpatients with obsessive compulsive disorder in the UK. International Journal of Psychiatry in Clinical Practice, 22(1), 54-62. https://pubmed.ncbi.nlm.nih.gov/28705096/

Meier, S. M., Petersen, L., Schendel, D. E., Mattheisen, M., Mortensen, P. B., & Mors, O. (2015). Obsessive-compulsive disorder and autism spectrum disorders: Longitudinal and offspring risk. PLOS ONE, 10(11), e0141703. https://pubmed.ncbi.nlm.nih.gov/26558765/

Russell, A. J., Jassi, A., Fullana, M. A., Mack, H., Johnston, K., Heyman, I., Murphy, D. G., & Mataix-Cols, D. (2013). Cognitive behavior therapy for comorbid obsessive-compulsive disorder in high-functioning autism spectrum disorders: A randomized controlled trial.

Depression and Anxiety, 30(8), 697-708. https://pubmed.ncbi.nlm.nih.gov/23389964/

Flygare, O., Andersson, E., Ringberg, H., Hellstadius, K., Edbacken, J., Enander, J., Ljotsson, B., Mataix-Cols, D., & Serlachius, E. (2020). Adapted cognitive behavior therapy for obsessive-compulsive disorder with co-occurring autism spectrum disorder: A clinical effectiveness study. Autism, 24(1), 190-199. https://pubmed.ncbi.nlm.nih.gov/31187645/

National Institute for Health and Care Excellence. (2005, surveillance updated 2019). Obsessive-compulsive disorder and body dysmorphic disorder: Treatment (CG31). https://www.nice.org.uk/guidance/cg31

Chapter 9 Rules and Mental Rituals

Nadia rehearses a phone call because spontaneous speech is hard. She also mentally replays a conversation 40 times to prove she did not lie. The outside view is simple: repetition. The inside story is not. A movement, question, sequence, or thought can be repeated for several reasons, and those reasons matter more than the photograph of the behavior. This chapter uses a composite scenario. Nadia's details are blended from common patterns described in the literature and are not a portrait of one real person.

Autism and OCD can both include repetition. Autism is defined in part by restricted or repetitive patterns of behavior, interests, or activities, while OCD involves obsessions, compulsions, or both (National Institute of Mental Health [NIMH], n.d.-a; National Institute of Mental Health [NIMH], n.d.-b). That overlap is exactly why appearance is a poor shortcut. The useful question is not simply, 'Is it repetitive?' It is, 'What job is the repetition doing?'

The Chapter Principle

Use the Four-Clue Overlap Map: trigger, function, interruption, and history. For internal repetition, an autism-related pattern may be connected with scripts, rehearsal, patterning, language processing, or planning. An OCD pattern is more likely when the act is recruited for silent checking, reviewing, counting, praying, replacing thoughts, or seeking a just-right feeling. None of these clues diagnoses anything by itself. Together they make a better clinical conversation.

Clue One Trigger

Start with what comes immediately before the behavior. A sensory demand, sudden transition, boredom, excitement, or need for focus can point toward regulation or predictability. A spike of doubt, contamination fear, moral fear, harm image, or 'what if' question can

point toward an OCD cycle. The same person can have both. The goal is to describe the sequence without deciding the label first.

Write the trigger as a camera could record it. 'The plan changed five minutes before we left' is better than 'I was triggered.' 'I noticed a thought that I might have left the stove on' is better than 'My anxiety got bad.' Concrete language lets a clinician ask the next question. Research comparing autism and OCD supports careful attention to phenomenology rather than assuming repetitive acts are equivalent (Cath et al., 2008; Santore et al., 2020).

Clue Two Function

Function means what the behavior is trying to change. Does it add useful sensation, organize attention, reduce overload, preserve a preferred pattern, or make an activity enjoyable? Those are different from trying to cancel danger, prove innocence, remove doubt, achieve a protective feeling, or satisfy a rule that says something bad will happen otherwise. In practice, mixed motives are common. You do not need a perfectly clean answer.

Ask a harder question: if there were no feared consequence at all, would you still want to do it? If the answer is yes because the act feels good, helps concentration, supports transition, or is part of a valued interest, that is information. If the answer is no, and the act feels like a tax paid to reduce threat or doubt, that is different information. Qualitative research with autistic adults who also have OCD describes how difficult and important this distinction can be (Long et al., 2024; Wikramanayake et al., 2018).

Clue Three Interruption

Interruption is not a morality test. Notice what kind of distress appears when the pattern is blocked. Sensory discomfort, disorganization, loss of focus, frustration at abrupt change, or a feeling of being neurologically overloaded can occur around autistic routines and

repetitive behavior. OCD interruption more often exposes the feared uncertainty the compulsion was managing: 'What if I did not check enough?' 'What if the contamination spreads?' 'What if this thought means I am dangerous?'

There is overlap here too. Autistic people can feel intense anxiety when a routine is interrupted, and people with OCD can describe bodily discomfort or a 'not just right' feeling rather than a clear catastrophic belief. That is why one clue never settles the question. The pattern across all four clues is more informative than any single answer.

Clue Four History

History asks when the pattern began and what else was true at the time. Autism is developmental, so a clinician assessing autism looks for a broader developmental pattern, not only current repetition. OCD can begin in childhood, adolescence, or adulthood and may wax and wane. A new ritual appearing after a period of intrusive doubt tells a different story from a lifelong preference for the same sensory input or sequence. Population and clinic studies show meaningful co-occurrence, so history should leave room for both rather than forcing an either-or answer (Meier et al., 2015; Wikramanayake et al., 2018).

If you can, collect examples from more than one age and setting. Old school reports, family recollections, childhood interests, early sensory patterns, and previous treatment responses can all be useful. Family memory is imperfect, and lack of documentation does not prove absence. Treat it as evidence to discuss, not a verdict.

A Worked Comparison

Take Nadia's situation and write two competing explanations. Explanation A: the behavior is mainly connected with scripts, rehearsal, patterning, language processing, or planning. Explanation B: the behavior is mainly connected with silent checking, reviewing, counting, praying, replacing thoughts, or seeking a just-right feeling. Now ask what each explanation predicts. If A is closer, accommodation or regulation may reduce distress without requiring the person to defeat a fear. If B is closer, reducing compulsive responding to feared uncertainty may be clinically relevant. If both predictions fit at different times, co-occurrence becomes a serious possibility.

This method prevents a common reasoning error: treating the name of an action as if it revealed its function. 'Checking,' 'repeating,' 'collecting,' 'researching,' and 'avoiding' are verbs, not diagnoses. A person can research a favorite topic for pleasure, research a feared disease for reassurance, or do both in the same evening. Ask what happened before, what the act was supposed to accomplish, and what happened after.

What Treatment Response Can Tell You

Treatment response is information, but it is not a home diagnostic test. ERP is an evidence-based component of CBT for OCD, and studies suggest adapted CBT can help autistic people who genuinely have co-occurring OCD (Russell et al., 2013; Flygare et al., 2020; National Institute for Health and Care Excellence [NICE], 2005/2019). That does not mean every repetitive autistic behavior should be targeted with exposure. If the target is sensory regulation, communication support, or a stable routine rather than an OCD compulsion, removing it can increase distress without treating the problem you meant to treat.

The safer principle is target accuracy. A clinician should identify the feared prediction or compulsive rule before asking you to resist a behavior as part of ERP. Adaptations may include clearer structure, concrete language, slower pacing, attention to sensory needs, and explicit differentiation between OCD goals and autism-related supports. If treatment repeatedly feels aimed at the wrong mechanism, bring that observation back to the clinician rather than trying to push through on principle.

What Appearance Gets Wrong

A quick label can hide mixed functions. With internal repetition, three mistakes are especially common. The first is assuming that visible anxiety proves OCD. A disrupted autistic routine or sensory overload can produce intense anxiety without a compulsion being present. The second is assuming that enjoyment rules OCD out. A person can feel temporary relief after a compulsion, and relief can be mistaken for preference. The third is assuming that a behavior has one function forever. A lifelong routine can later become entangled with OCD, or a person can begin using a familiar autistic behavior as part of a new threat-reduction rule.

For that reason, describe episodes rather than traits whenever you can. Instead of writing, "I always do this because I am autistic," record one recent example. Instead of writing, "This is definitely OCD," record the feared possibility, the rule, and what the behavior was supposed to prevent. Good differential assessment is built from patterns across examples. It is also allowed to end with more than one explanation.

Questions to Take to a Clinician

Bring examples instead of conclusions. Useful questions include: 'What makes you think this behavior is a compulsion rather than a regulating repetitive behavior?' 'What feared outcome or uncertainty are we targeting?' 'How are you accounting for sensory needs and developmental history?' 'Could both autism and OCD be present?' 'How will we know whether this intervention is reducing OCD rather than simply increasing my tolerance of distress from losing a useful support?'

A good assessment is not a debate you have to win. It is a process of making the evidence visible. You can help by naming the sequence precisely: what happened, what you thought or sensed, what you did,

what you hoped the act would change, and what happened next. That gives a clinician something more useful than a checklist score alone.

Try the Four-Clue Overlap Map

Choose one example of internal repetition. On one page, make four headings: Trigger, Function, Interruption, History. Under Trigger, record what came first. Under Function, record what the behavior was meant to change. Under Interruption, record the kind of distress that appears if you stop. Under History, record when the pattern first appeared and whether it has changed. Add a final line called 'What I am not sure about.' That last line is often the most useful one to bring to assessment.

Principles to Remember

The visible behavior is the beginning of the question, not the answer. For internal repetition, look at trigger, function, interruption, and history before assigning meaning. Autism-related repetition can be valuable, regulating, pleasurable, or stabilizing. OCD compulsions are typically recruited into a cycle of threat, doubt, or rule-driven relief. Some experiences sit between those descriptions, and some people have both conditions. Your task is not to diagnose yourself from one clue. It is to build a clearer account of what is happening so the right professional questions can be asked.

References

National Institute of Mental Health. (n.d.-a). Autism spectrum disorder. https://www.nimh.nih.gov/health/publications/autism-spectrum-disorder

National Institute of Mental Health. (n.d.-b). Obsessive-compulsive disorder. https://www.nimh.nih.gov/health/topics/obsessive-compulsive-disorder-ocd

Cath, D. C., Ran, N., Smit, J. H., van Balkom, A. J. L. M., & Comijs, H. C. (2008). Symptom overlap between autism spectrum disorder, generalized social anxiety disorder and obsessive-compulsive disorder in adults: A preliminary case-controlled study. Psychopathology, 41(2), 101-110. https://pubmed.ncbi.nlm.nih.gov/18033980/

Santore, L. A., Gerber, A. H., Gioia, A. N., Bianchi, R., Talledo, F., Peris, T. S., & Lerner, M. D. (2020). Felt but not seen: Observed restricted repetitive behaviors are associated with self-report but not parent-report obsessive-compulsive disorder symptoms in youth with autism. Autism, 24(4), 983-994. https://pmc.ncbi.nlm.nih.gov/articles/PMC7337249/

Long, H. A., Rodgers, J., & South, M. (2024). 'Autism is the arena and OCD is the lion': Autistic adults' experiences of co-occurring obsessive-compulsive disorder. Autism. https://pmc.ncbi.nlm.nih.gov/articles/PMC11497754/

Wikramanayake, W. N. M., Mandy, W., Shahper, S., Kaur, S., Kolli, S., Osman, S., Reid, J., Jefferies-Sewell, K., & Fineberg, N. A. (2018). Autism spectrum disorders in adult outpatients with obsessive compulsive disorder in the UK. International Journal of Psychiatry in Clinical Practice, 22(1), 54-62. https://pubmed.ncbi.nlm.nih.gov/28705096/

Meier, S. M., Petersen, L., Schendel, D. E., Mattheisen, M., Mortensen, P. B., & Mors, O. (2015). Obsessive-compulsive disorder and autism spectrum disorders: Longitudinal and offspring risk. PLOS ONE, 10(11), e0141703. https://pubmed.ncbi.nlm.nih.gov/26558765/

Russell, A. J., Jassi, A., Fullana, M. A., Mack, H., Johnston, K., Heyman, I., Murphy, D. G., & Mataix-Cols, D. (2013). Cognitive behavior therapy for comorbid obsessive-compulsive disorder in high-functioning autism spectrum disorders: A randomized controlled trial. Depression and Anxiety, 30(8), 697-708. https://pubmed.ncbi.nlm.nih.gov/23389964/

Flygare, O., Andersson, E., Ringberg, H., Hellstadius, K., Edbacken, J., Enander, J., Ljotsson, B., Mataix-Cols, D., & Serlachius,

E. (2020). Adapted cognitive behavior therapy for obsessive-compulsive disorder with co-occurring autism spectrum disorder: A clinical effectiveness study. Autism, 24(1), 190-199. https://pubmed.ncbi.nlm.nih.gov/31187645/

National Institute for Health and Care Excellence. (2005, surveillance updated 2019). Obsessive-compulsive disorder and body dysmorphic disorder: Treatment (CG31). https://www.nice.org.uk/guidance/cg31

Chapter 10 Reassurance and Research Loops

Research can be a pleasure, a practical tool, or a compulsion, and the browser history will not tell you which. Marcus spends hours reading about a favorite technical subject because he enjoys the detail. On a different night he searches the same health question again and again, hoping one more page will finally make him feel certain. The outside view is simple: repetition. The inside story is not. A movement, question, sequence, or thought can be repeated for several reasons, and those reasons matter more than the photograph of the behavior. This chapter uses a composite scenario. Marcus's details are blended from common patterns described in the literature and are not a portrait of one real person.

Autism and OCD can both include repetition. Autism is defined in part by restricted or repetitive patterns of behavior, interests, or activities, while OCD involves obsessions, compulsions, or both (National Institute of Mental Health [NIMH], n.d.-a; National Institute of Mental Health [NIMH], n.d.-b). That overlap is exactly why appearance is a poor shortcut. The useful question is not simply, 'Is it repetitive?' It is, 'What job is the repetition doing?'

The Chapter Principle

Use the Four-Clue Overlap Map: trigger, function, interruption, and history. For repeated asking, searching, or researching, an autism-related pattern may be connected with gathering information for interest, planning, communication, or genuine problem solving. An OCD pattern is more likely when the act is recruited for trying to obtain enough reassurance to make feared uncertainty disappear. None of these clues diagnoses anything by itself. Together they make a better clinical conversation.

Clue One Trigger

Start with what comes immediately before the behavior. A sensory demand, sudden transition, boredom, excitement, or need for focus can point toward regulation or predictability. A spike of doubt, contamination fear, moral fear, harm image, or 'what if' question can point toward an OCD cycle. The same person can have both. The goal is to describe the sequence without deciding the label first.

Write the trigger as a camera could record it. 'The plan changed five minutes before we left' is better than 'I was triggered.' 'I noticed a thought that I might have left the stove on' is better than 'My anxiety got bad.' Concrete language lets a clinician ask the next question. Research comparing autism and OCD supports careful attention to phenomenology rather than assuming repetitive acts are equivalent (Cath et al., 2008; Santore et al., 2020).

Clue Two Function

Function means what the behavior is trying to change. Does it add useful sensation, organize attention, reduce overload, preserve a preferred pattern, or make an activity enjoyable? Those are different from trying to cancel danger, prove innocence, remove doubt, achieve a protective feeling, or satisfy a rule that says something bad will happen otherwise. In practice, mixed motives are common. You do not need a perfectly clean answer.

Ask a harder question: if there were no feared consequence at all, would you still want to do it? If the answer is yes because the act feels good, helps concentration, supports transition, or is part of a valued interest, that is information. If the answer is no, and the act feels like a tax paid to reduce threat or doubt, that is different information. Qualitative research with autistic adults who also have OCD describes how difficult and important this distinction can be (Long et al., 2024; Wikramanayake et al., 2018).

Clue Three Interruption

Interruption is not a morality test. Notice what kind of distress appears when the pattern is blocked. Sensory discomfort, disorganization, loss of focus, frustration at abrupt change, or a feeling of being neurologically overloaded can occur around autistic routines and repetitive behavior. OCD interruption more often exposes the feared uncertainty the compulsion was managing: 'What if I did not check enough?' 'What if the contamination spreads?' 'What if this thought means I am dangerous?'

There is overlap here too. Autistic people can feel intense anxiety when a routine is interrupted, and people with OCD can describe bodily discomfort or a 'not just right' feeling rather than a clear catastrophic belief. That is why one clue never settles the question. The pattern across all four clues is more informative than any single answer.

Clue Four History

History asks when the pattern began and what else was true at the time. Autism is developmental, so a clinician assessing autism looks for a broader developmental pattern, not only current repetition. OCD can begin in childhood, adolescence, or adulthood and may wax and wane. A new ritual appearing after a period of intrusive doubt tells a different story from a lifelong preference for the same sensory input or sequence. Population and clinic studies show meaningful co-occurrence, so history should leave room for both rather than forcing an either-or answer (Meier et al., 2015; Wikramanayake et al., 2018).

If you can, collect examples from more than one age and setting. Old school reports, family recollections, childhood interests, early sensory patterns, and previous treatment responses can all be useful. Family memory is imperfect, and lack of documentation does not prove absence. Treat it as evidence to discuss, not a verdict.

A Worked Comparison

Take Marcus's situation and write two competing explanations. Explanation A: the behavior is mainly connected with gathering information for interest, planning, communication, or genuine problem solving. Explanation B: the behavior is mainly connected with trying to obtain enough reassurance to make feared uncertainty disappear. Now ask what each explanation predicts. If A is closer, accommodation or regulation may reduce distress without requiring the person to defeat a fear. If B is closer, reducing compulsive responding to feared uncertainty may be clinically relevant. If both predictions fit at different times, co-occurrence becomes a serious possibility.

This method prevents a common reasoning error: treating the name of an action as if it revealed its function. 'Checking,' 'repeating,' 'collecting,' 'researching,' and 'avoiding' are verbs, not diagnoses. A person can research a favorite topic for pleasure, research a feared disease for reassurance, or do both in the same evening. Ask what happened before, what the act was supposed to accomplish, and what happened after.

What Treatment Response Can Tell You

Treatment response is information, but it is not a home diagnostic test. ERP is an evidence-based component of CBT for OCD, and studies suggest adapted CBT can help autistic people who genuinely have co-occurring OCD (Russell et al., 2013; Flygare et al., 2020; National Institute for Health and Care Excellence [NICE], 2005/2019). That does not mean every repetitive autistic behavior should be targeted with exposure. If the target is sensory regulation, communication support, or a stable routine rather than an OCD compulsion, removing it can increase distress without treating the problem you meant to treat.

The safer principle is target accuracy. A clinician should identify the feared prediction or compulsive rule before asking you to resist a behavior as part of ERP. Adaptations may include clearer structure, concrete language, slower pacing, attention to sensory needs, and explicit differentiation between OCD goals and autism-related supports. If treatment repeatedly feels aimed at the wrong mechanism, bring that observation back to the clinician rather than trying to push through on principle.

What Appearance Gets Wrong

A quick label can hide mixed functions. With repeated asking, searching, or researching, three mistakes are especially common. The first is assuming that visible anxiety proves OCD. A disrupted autistic routine or sensory overload can produce intense anxiety without a compulsion being present. The second is assuming that enjoyment rules OCD out. A person can feel temporary relief after a compulsion, and relief can be mistaken for preference. The third is assuming that a behavior has one function forever. A lifelong routine can later become entangled with OCD, or a person can begin using a familiar autistic behavior as part of a new threat-reduction rule.

For that reason, describe episodes rather than traits whenever you can. Instead of writing, "I always do this because I am autistic," record one recent example. Instead of writing, "This is definitely OCD," record the feared possibility, the rule, and what the behavior was supposed to prevent. Good differential assessment is built from patterns across examples. It is also allowed to end with more than one explanation.

Questions to Take to a Clinician

Bring examples instead of conclusions. Useful questions include: 'What makes you think this behavior is a compulsion rather than a regulating repetitive behavior?' 'What feared outcome or uncertainty are we targeting?' 'How are you accounting for sensory needs and developmental history?' 'Could both autism and OCD be present?'

'How will we know whether this intervention is reducing OCD rather than simply increasing my tolerance of distress from losing a useful support?'

A good assessment is not a debate you have to win. It is a process of making the evidence visible. You can help by naming the sequence precisely: what happened, what you thought or sensed, what you did, what you hoped the act would change, and what happened next. That gives a clinician something more useful than a checklist score alone.

Try the Four-Clue Overlap Map

Choose one example of repeated asking, searching, or researching. On one page, make four headings: Trigger, Function, Interruption, History. Under Trigger, record what came first. Under Function, record what the behavior was meant to change. Under Interruption, record the kind of distress that appears if you stop. Under History, record when the pattern first appeared and whether it has changed. Add a final line called 'What I am not sure about.' That last line is often the most useful one to bring to assessment.

In a Nutshell

The visible behavior is the beginning of the question, not the answer. For repeated asking, searching, or researching, look at trigger, function, interruption, and history before assigning meaning. Autism-related repetition can be valuable, regulating, pleasurable, or stabilizing. OCD compulsions are typically recruited into a cycle of threat, doubt, or rule-driven relief. Some experiences sit between those descriptions, and some people have both conditions. Your task is not to diagnose yourself from one clue. It is to build a clearer account of what is happening so the right professional questions can be asked.

References

National Institute of Mental Health. (n.d.-a). Autism spectrum disorder. https://www.nimh.nih.gov/health/publications/autism-spectrum-disorder

National Institute of Mental Health. (n.d.-b). Obsessive-compulsive disorder. https://www.nimh.nih.gov/health/topics/obsessive-compulsive-disorder-ocd

Cath, D. C., Ran, N., Smit, J. H., van Balkom, A. J. L. M., & Comijs, H. C. (2008). Symptom overlap between autism spectrum disorder, generalized social anxiety disorder and obsessive-compulsive disorder in adults: A preliminary case-controlled study. Psychopathology, 41(2), 101-110. https://pubmed.ncbi.nlm.nih.gov/18033980/

Santore, L. A., Gerber, A. H., Gioia, A. N., Bianchi, R., Talledo, F., Peris, T. S., & Lerner, M. D. (2020). Felt but not seen: Observed restricted repetitive behaviors are associated with self-report but not parent-report obsessive-compulsive disorder symptoms in youth with autism. Autism, 24(4), 983-994. https://pmc.ncbi.nlm.nih.gov/articles/PMC7337249/

Long, H. A., Rodgers, J., & South, M. (2024). 'Autism is the arena and OCD is the lion': Autistic adults' experiences of co-occurring obsessive-compulsive disorder. Autism. https://pmc.ncbi.nlm.nih.gov/articles/PMC11497754/

Wikramanayake, W. N. M., Mandy, W., Shahper, S., Kaur, S., Kolli, S., Osman, S., Reid, J., Jefferies-Sewell, K., & Fineberg, N. A. (2018). Autism spectrum disorders in adult outpatients with obsessive compulsive disorder in the UK. International Journal of Psychiatry in Clinical Practice, 22(1), 54-62. https://pubmed.ncbi.nlm.nih.gov/28705096/

Meier, S. M., Petersen, L., Schendel, D. E., Mattheisen, M., Mortensen, P. B., & Mors, O. (2015). Obsessive-compulsive disorder

and autism spectrum disorders: Longitudinal and offspring risk. PLOS ONE, 10(11), e0141703. https://pubmed.ncbi.nlm.nih.gov/26558765/

Russell, A. J., Jassi, A., Fullana, M. A., Mack, H., Johnston, K., Heyman, I., Murphy, D. G., & Mataix-Cols, D. (2013). Cognitive behavior therapy for comorbid obsessive-compulsive disorder in high-functioning autism spectrum disorders: A randomized controlled trial. Depression and Anxiety, 30(8), 697-708. https://pubmed.ncbi.nlm.nih.gov/23389964/

Flygare, O., Andersson, E., Ringberg, H., Hellstadius, K., Edbacken, J., Enander, J., Ljotsson, B., Mataix-Cols, D., & Serlachius, E. (2020). Adapted cognitive behavior therapy for obsessive-compulsive disorder with co-occurring autism spectrum disorder: A clinical effectiveness study. Autism, 24(1), 190-199. https://pubmed.ncbi.nlm.nih.gov/31187645/

National Institute for Health and Care Excellence. (2005, surveillance updated 2019). Obsessive-compulsive disorder and body dysmorphic disorder: Treatment (CG31). https://www.nice.org.uk/guidance/cg31

Chapter 11 When Both Are Present

Owen has always needed warning before schedule changes. Later, OCD adds a rule that every change must be preceded by a specific checking sequence. The outside view is simple: repetition. The inside story is not. A movement, question, sequence, or thought can be repeated for several reasons, and those reasons matter more than the photograph of the behavior. This chapter uses a composite scenario. Owen's details are blended from common patterns described in the literature and are not a portrait of one real person.

Autism and OCD can both include repetition. Autism is defined in part by restricted or repetitive patterns of behavior, interests, or activities, while OCD involves obsessions, compulsions, or both (National Institute of Mental Health [NIMH], n.d.-a; National Institute of Mental Health [NIMH], n.d.-b). That overlap is exactly why appearance is a poor shortcut. The useful question is not simply, 'Is it repetitive?' It is, 'What job is the repetition doing?'

The Chapter Principle

Use the Four-Clue Overlap Map: trigger, function, interruption, and history. For co-occurrence, an autism-related pattern may be connected with autism can shape how OCD is experienced and communicated. An OCD pattern is more likely when the act is recruited for OCD can attach itself to autistic routines, interests, rules, and sensory concerns. None of these clues diagnoses anything by itself. Together they make a better clinical conversation.

Clue One Trigger

Start with what comes immediately before the behavior. A sensory demand, sudden transition, boredom, excitement, or need for focus can point toward regulation or predictability. A spike of doubt, contamination fear, moral fear, harm image, or 'what if' question can

point toward an OCD cycle. The same person can have both. The goal is to describe the sequence without deciding the label first.

Write the trigger as a camera could record it. 'The plan changed five minutes before we left' is better than 'I was triggered.' 'I noticed a thought that I might have left the stove on' is better than 'My anxiety got bad.' Concrete language lets a clinician ask the next question. Research comparing autism and OCD supports careful attention to phenomenology rather than assuming repetitive acts are equivalent (Cath et al., 2008; Santore et al., 2020).

Clue Two Function

Function means what the behavior is trying to change. Does it add useful sensation, organize attention, reduce overload, preserve a preferred pattern, or make an activity enjoyable? Those are different from trying to cancel danger, prove innocence, remove doubt, achieve a protective feeling, or satisfy a rule that says something bad will happen otherwise. In practice, mixed motives are common. You do not need a perfectly clean answer.

Ask a harder question: if there were no feared consequence at all, would you still want to do it? If the answer is yes because the act feels good, helps concentration, supports transition, or is part of a valued interest, that is information. If the answer is no, and the act feels like a tax paid to reduce threat or doubt, that is different information. Qualitative research with autistic adults who also have OCD describes how difficult and important this distinction can be (Long et al., 2024; Wikramanayake et al., 2018).

Clue Three Interruption

Interruption is not a morality test. Notice what kind of distress appears when the pattern is blocked. Sensory discomfort, disorganization, loss of focus, frustration at abrupt change, or a feeling of being neurologically overloaded can occur around autistic routines and

repetitive behavior. OCD interruption more often exposes the feared uncertainty the compulsion was managing: 'What if I did not check enough?' 'What if the contamination spreads?' 'What if this thought means I am dangerous?'

There is overlap here too. Autistic people can feel intense anxiety when a routine is interrupted, and people with OCD can describe bodily discomfort or a 'not just right' feeling rather than a clear catastrophic belief. That is why one clue never settles the question. The pattern across all four clues is more informative than any single answer.

Clue Four History

History asks when the pattern began and what else was true at the time. Autism is developmental, so a clinician assessing autism looks for a broader developmental pattern, not only current repetition. OCD can begin in childhood, adolescence, or adulthood and may wax and wane. A new ritual appearing after a period of intrusive doubt tells a different story from a lifelong preference for the same sensory input or sequence. Population and clinic studies show meaningful co-occurrence, so history should leave room for both rather than forcing an either-or answer (Meier et al., 2015; Wikramanayake et al., 2018).

If you can, collect examples from more than one age and setting. Old school reports, family recollections, childhood interests, early sensory patterns, and previous treatment responses can all be useful. Family memory is imperfect, and lack of documentation does not prove absence. Treat it as evidence to discuss, not a verdict.

A Worked Comparison

Take Owen's situation and write two competing explanations. Explanation A: the behavior is mainly connected with autism can shape how OCD is experienced and communicated. Explanation B: the behavior is mainly connected with OCD can attach itself to autistic routines, interests, rules, and sensory concerns. Now ask what each explanation predicts. If A is closer, accommodation or regulation may reduce distress without requiring the person to defeat a fear. If B is closer, reducing compulsive responding to feared uncertainty may be clinically relevant. If both predictions fit at different times, co-occurrence becomes a serious possibility.

This method prevents a common reasoning error: treating the name of an action as if it revealed its function. 'Checking,' 'repeating,' 'collecting,' 'researching,' and 'avoiding' are verbs, not diagnoses. A person can research a favorite topic for pleasure, research a feared disease for reassurance, or do both in the same evening. Ask what happened before, what the act was supposed to accomplish, and what happened after.

What Treatment Response Can Tell You

Treatment response is information, but it is not a home diagnostic test. ERP is an evidence-based component of CBT for OCD, and studies suggest adapted CBT can help autistic people who genuinely have co-occurring OCD (Russell et al., 2013; Flygare et al., 2020; National Institute for Health and Care Excellence [NICE], 2005/2019). That does not mean every repetitive autistic behavior should be targeted with exposure. If the target is sensory regulation, communication support, or a stable routine rather than an OCD compulsion, removing it can increase distress without treating the problem you meant to treat.

The safer principle is target accuracy. A clinician should identify the feared prediction or compulsive rule before asking you to resist a behavior as part of ERP. Adaptations may include clearer structure, concrete language, slower pacing, attention to sensory needs, and explicit differentiation between OCD goals and autism-related supports. If treatment repeatedly feels aimed at the wrong mechanism, bring that observation back to the clinician rather than trying to push through on principle.

What Appearance Gets Wrong

A quick label can hide mixed functions. With co-occurrence, three mistakes are especially common. The first is assuming that visible anxiety proves OCD. A disrupted autistic routine or sensory overload can produce intense anxiety without a compulsion being present. The second is assuming that enjoyment rules OCD out. A person can feel temporary relief after a compulsion, and relief can be mistaken for preference. The third is assuming that a behavior has one function forever. A lifelong routine can later become entangled with OCD, or a person can begin using a familiar autistic behavior as part of a new threat-reduction rule.

For that reason, describe episodes rather than traits whenever you can. Instead of writing, "I always do this because I am autistic," record one recent example. Instead of writing, "This is definitely OCD," record the feared possibility, the rule, and what the behavior was supposed to prevent. Good differential assessment is built from patterns across examples. It is also allowed to end with more than one explanation.

Co-occurrence Changes the Formulation

When autism and OCD occur together, the clinical task is not to decide which diagnosis gets ownership of every repeated behavior. It is to identify which patterns belong to developmental autistic traits, which belong to OCD, and where OCD has attached itself to an existing routine or interest.

That attachment can be subtle. A person may have used a predictable bedtime sequence for years because transitions are easier when the order is stable. Later, OCD can add a rule that the sequence must be restarted if a particular thought occurs. The original routine did not become fake. A new compulsive layer appeared on top of it. Treatment can then target the added rule while preserving the useful structure underneath.

The reverse problem also occurs. A clinician may see a person with a known OCD diagnosis and interpret every repeated action through that lens, missing longstanding sensory needs, social-communication differences, and focused interests. Or an autism diagnosis may become the explanation for checking and reassurance that are consuming hours. Co-occurrence asks for a formulation that can hold more than one mechanism at once. That is slower than choosing a single label, but it is closer to how many real cases are organized.

Questions to Take to a Clinician

Bring examples instead of conclusions. Useful questions include: 'What makes you think this behavior is a compulsion rather than a regulating repetitive behavior?' 'What feared outcome or uncertainty are we targeting?' 'How are you accounting for sensory needs and developmental history?' 'Could both autism and OCD be present?' 'How will we know whether this intervention is reducing OCD rather than simply increasing my tolerance of distress from losing a useful support?'

A good assessment is not a debate you have to win. It is a process of making the evidence visible. You can help by naming the sequence precisely: what happened, what you thought or sensed, what you did, what you hoped the act would change, and what happened next. That gives a clinician something more useful than a checklist score alone.

Try the Four-Clue Overlap Map

Choose one example of co-occurrence. On one page, make four headings: Trigger, Function, Interruption, History. Under Trigger, record what came first. Under Function, record what the behavior was meant to change. Under Interruption, record the kind of distress that appears if you stop. Under History, record when the pattern first appeared and whether it has changed. Add a final line called 'What I am not sure about.' That last line is often the most useful one to bring to assessment.

Principles to Remember

The visible behavior is the beginning of the question, not the answer. For co-occurrence, look at trigger, function, interruption, and history before assigning meaning. Autism-related repetition can be valuable, regulating, pleasurable, or stabilizing. OCD compulsions are typically recruited into a cycle of threat, doubt, or rule-driven relief. Some experiences sit between those descriptions, and some people have both conditions. Your task is not to diagnose yourself from one clue. It is to build a clearer account of what is happening so the right professional questions can be asked.

References

National Institute of Mental Health. (n.d.-a). Autism spectrum disorder. https://www.nimh.nih.gov/health/publications/autism-spectrum-disorder

National Institute of Mental Health. (n.d.-b). Obsessive-compulsive disorder. https://www.nimh.nih.gov/health/topics/obsessive-compulsive-disorder-ocd

Cath, D. C., Ran, N., Smit, J. H., van Balkom, A. J. L. M., & Comijs, H. C. (2008). Symptom overlap between autism spectrum disorder, generalized social anxiety disorder and obsessive-compulsive disorder in adults: A preliminary case-controlled study. Psychopathology, 41(2), 101-110. https://pubmed.ncbi.nlm.nih.gov/18033980/

Santore, L. A., Gerber, A. H., Gioia, A. N., Bianchi, R., Talledo, F., Peris, T. S., & Lerner, M. D. (2020). Felt but not seen: Observed restricted repetitive behaviors are associated with self-report but not parent-report obsessive-compulsive disorder symptoms in youth with autism. Autism, 24(4), 983-994. https://pmc.ncbi.nlm.nih.gov/articles/PMC7337249/

Long, H. A., Rodgers, J., & South, M. (2024). 'Autism is the arena and OCD is the lion': Autistic adults' experiences of co-occurring obsessive-compulsive disorder. Autism. https://pmc.ncbi.nlm.nih.gov/articles/PMC11497754/

Wikramanayake, W. N. M., Mandy, W., Shahper, S., Kaur, S., Kolli, S., Osman, S., Reid, J., Jefferies-Sewell, K., & Fineberg, N. A. (2018). Autism spectrum disorders in adult outpatients with obsessive compulsive disorder in the UK. International Journal of Psychiatry in Clinical Practice, 22(1), 54-62. https://pubmed.ncbi.nlm.nih.gov/28705096/

Meier, S. M., Petersen, L., Schendel, D. E., Mattheisen, M., Mortensen, P. B., & Mors, O. (2015). Obsessive-compulsive disorder and autism spectrum disorders: Longitudinal and offspring risk. PLOS ONE, 10(11), e0141703. https://pubmed.ncbi.nlm.nih.gov/26558765/

Russell, A. J., Jassi, A., Fullana, M. A., Mack, H., Johnston, K., Heyman, I., Murphy, D. G., & Mataix-Cols, D. (2013). Cognitive behavior therapy for comorbid obsessive-compulsive disorder in high-functioning autism spectrum disorders: A randomized controlled trial. Depression and Anxiety, 30(8), 697-708. https://pubmed.ncbi.nlm.nih.gov/23389964/

Flygare, O., Andersson, E., Ringberg, H., Hellstadius, K., Edbacken, J., Enander, J., Ljotsson, B., Mataix-Cols, D., & Serlachius, E. (2020). Adapted cognitive behavior therapy for obsessive-compulsive disorder with co-occurring autism spectrum disorder: A clinical effectiveness study. Autism, 24(1), 190-199. https://pubmed.ncbi.nlm.nih.gov/31187645/

National Institute for Health and Care Excellence. (2005, surveillance updated 2019). Obsessive-compulsive disorder and body dysmorphic disorder: Treatment (CG31). https://www.nice.org.uk/guidance/cg31

Chapter 12 Treatment Fit Matters

Treatment only makes sense when the target has been named correctly. Amina is told to stop every repetitive behavior as an exposure exercise. Her distress rises, but the target was a regulating movement rather than an OCD compulsion. The outside view is simple: repetition. The inside story is not. A movement, question, sequence, or thought can be repeated for several reasons, and those reasons matter more than the photograph of the behavior. This chapter uses a composite scenario. Amina's details are blended from common patterns described in the literature and are not a portrait of one real person.

Autism and OCD can both include repetition. Autism is defined in part by restricted or repetitive patterns of behavior, interests, or activities, while OCD involves obsessions, compulsions, or both (National Institute of Mental Health [NIMH], n.d.-a; National Institute of Mental Health [NIMH], n.d.-b). That overlap is exactly why appearance is a poor shortcut. The useful question is not simply, 'Is it repetitive?' It is, 'What job is the repetition doing?'

The Chapter Principle

Use the Four-Clue Overlap Map: trigger, function, interruption, and history. For intervention choice, an autism-related pattern may be connected with supporting sensory regulation and useful routines. An OCD pattern is more likely when the act is recruited for using evidence-based OCD treatment for genuine obsessions and compulsions, adapted when needed. None of these clues diagnoses anything by itself. Together they make a better clinical conversation.

Clue One Trigger

Start with what comes immediately before the behavior. A sensory demand, sudden transition, boredom, excitement, or need for focus can

point toward regulation or predictability. A spike of doubt, contamination fear, moral fear, harm image, or 'what if' question can point toward an OCD cycle. The same person can have both. The goal is to describe the sequence without deciding the label first.

Write the trigger as a camera could record it. 'The plan changed five minutes before we left' is better than 'I was triggered.' 'I noticed a thought that I might have left the stove on' is better than 'My anxiety got bad.' Concrete language lets a clinician ask the next question. Research comparing autism and OCD supports careful attention to phenomenology rather than assuming repetitive acts are equivalent (Cath et al., 2008; Santore et al., 2020).

Clue Two Function

Function means what the behavior is trying to change. Does it add useful sensation, organize attention, reduce overload, preserve a preferred pattern, or make an activity enjoyable? Those are different from trying to cancel danger, prove innocence, remove doubt, achieve a protective feeling, or satisfy a rule that says something bad will happen otherwise. In practice, mixed motives are common. You do not need a perfectly clean answer.

Ask a harder question: if there were no feared consequence at all, would you still want to do it? If the answer is yes because the act feels good, helps concentration, supports transition, or is part of a valued interest, that is information. If the answer is no, and the act feels like a tax paid to reduce threat or doubt, that is different information. Qualitative research with autistic adults who also have OCD describes how difficult and important this distinction can be (Long et al., 2024; Wikramanayake et al., 2018).

Clue Three Interruption

Interruption is not a morality test. Notice what kind of distress appears when the pattern is blocked. Sensory discomfort, disorganization, loss

of focus, frustration at abrupt change, or a feeling of being neurologically overloaded can occur around autistic routines and repetitive behavior. OCD interruption more often exposes the feared uncertainty the compulsion was managing: 'What if I did not check enough?' 'What if the contamination spreads?' 'What if this thought means I am dangerous?'

There is overlap here too. Autistic people can feel intense anxiety when a routine is interrupted, and people with OCD can describe bodily discomfort or a 'not just right' feeling rather than a clear catastrophic belief. That is why one clue never settles the question. The pattern across all four clues is more informative than any single answer.

Clue Four History

History asks when the pattern began and what else was true at the time. Autism is developmental, so a clinician assessing autism looks for a broader developmental pattern, not only current repetition. OCD can begin in childhood, adolescence, or adulthood and may wax and wane. A new ritual appearing after a period of intrusive doubt tells a different story from a lifelong preference for the same sensory input or sequence. Population and clinic studies show meaningful co-occurrence, so history should leave room for both rather than forcing an either-or answer (Meier et al., 2015; Wikramanayake et al., 2018).

If you can, collect examples from more than one age and setting. Old school reports, family recollections, childhood interests, early sensory patterns, and previous treatment responses can all be useful. Family memory is imperfect, and lack of documentation does not prove absence. Treat it as evidence to discuss, not a verdict.

A Worked Comparison

Take Amina's situation and write two competing explanations. Explanation A: the behavior is mainly connected with supporting sensory regulation and useful routines. Explanation B: the behavior is mainly connected with using evidence-based OCD treatment for genuine obsessions and compulsions, adapted when needed. Now ask what each explanation predicts. If A is closer, accommodation or regulation may reduce distress without requiring the person to defeat a fear. If B is closer, reducing compulsive responding to feared uncertainty may be clinically relevant. If both predictions fit at different times, co-occurrence becomes a serious possibility.

This method prevents a common reasoning error: treating the name of an action as if it revealed its function. 'Checking,' 'repeating,' 'collecting,' 'researching,' and 'avoiding' are verbs, not diagnoses. A person can research a favorite topic for pleasure, research a feared disease for reassurance, or do both in the same evening. Ask what happened before, what the act was supposed to accomplish, and what happened after.

What Treatment Response Can Tell You

Treatment response is information, but it is not a home diagnostic test. ERP is an evidence-based component of CBT for OCD, and studies suggest adapted CBT can help autistic people who genuinely have co-occurring OCD (Russell et al., 2013; Flygare et al., 2020; National Institute for Health and Care Excellence [NICE], 2005/2019). That does not mean every repetitive autistic behavior should be targeted with exposure. If the target is sensory regulation, communication support, or a stable routine rather than an OCD compulsion, removing it can increase distress without treating the problem you meant to treat.

The safer principle is target accuracy. A clinician should identify the feared prediction or compulsive rule before asking you to resist a behavior as part of ERP. Adaptations may include clearer structure, concrete language, slower pacing, attention to sensory needs, and explicit differentiation between OCD goals and autism-related supports. If treatment repeatedly feels aimed at the wrong mechanism,

bring that observation back to the clinician rather than trying to push through on principle.

What Appearance Gets Wrong

A quick label can hide mixed functions. With intervention choice, three mistakes are especially common. The first is assuming that visible anxiety proves OCD. A disrupted autistic routine or sensory overload can produce intense anxiety without a compulsion being present. The second is assuming that enjoyment rules OCD out. A person can feel temporary relief after a compulsion, and relief can be mistaken for preference. The third is assuming that a behavior has one function forever. A lifelong routine can later become entangled with OCD, or a person can begin using a familiar autistic behavior as part of a new threat-reduction rule.

For that reason, describe episodes rather than traits whenever you can. Instead of writing, "I always do this because I am autistic," record one recent example. Instead of writing, "This is definitely OCD," record the feared possibility, the rule, and what the behavior was supposed to prevent. Good differential assessment is built from patterns across examples. It is also allowed to end with more than one explanation.

Target Accuracy Comes Before Exposure

ERP works by helping a person approach feared cues or uncertainty while reducing the compulsive response that normally follows. That logic depends on identifying the OCD cycle correctly. If the behavior being removed is not functioning as a compulsion, the exercise may produce distress without testing the prediction ERP was designed to test.

Before an exposure task, ask for the target in one sentence. What is the feared prediction? What compulsion or safety behavior is being reduced? What learning is the exercise meant to make possible? If those questions cannot be answered, the plan may need clarification.

Autism-informed adaptation does not mean making OCD treatment so comfortable that no learning occurs. It means avoiding unnecessary barriers that are unrelated to the OCD target. Concrete language, predictable session structure, explicit rationale, attention to sensory load, and enough processing time can make the treatment more usable. The evidence base for adapted CBT in autistic people with OCD is smaller than the general OCD evidence base, but existing studies support the feasibility and potential value of adaptation. The practical point is precise: preserve supports that are not part of the compulsion unless there is a clear reason to change them, and make sure the difficult part of ERP is difficult for the reason you intend.

A Treatment Planning Conversation

A useful treatment conversation is concrete enough that you can tell what is being changed and what is being protected. Suppose an autistic adult has a morning routine, a contamination fear, and a sensory aversion to a particular cleaning product. A weak plan might describe all three as rigidity and ask the person to become more flexible. A stronger plan separates them. The routine may stay because it reduces decision load. The sensory aversion may be accommodated with a different product. The contamination compulsion may become the ERP target because it is linked to a feared consequence and repetitive washing.

That separation also makes progress easier to measure. If the person washes less because the feared contamination rule is loosening, that is relevant OCD change. If the person is simply more exhausted because a regulating routine was removed, distress alone does not show that ERP is working. Exposure is not graded by how miserable it makes someone. It is graded by whether the planned learning task is being completed and whether compulsive responding is changing over time.

Ask how the clinician will distinguish expected treatment discomfort from signs that the formulation needs revision. Expected discomfort may include anxiety, doubt, urges to ritualize, and the frustration of not obtaining certainty. A formulation problem may show up when the exercise repeatedly targets sensory pain, communication difficulty, or useful predictability with no identifiable obsession or compulsive rule. Those are not automatic stop signs, but they are reasons to revisit the target.

If a treatment plan includes several goals, write each one in mechanism language. "Touch the door handle and delay washing for 10 minutes to practice allowing contamination uncertainty" is more precise than "be less rigid about germs." "Keep the same appointment structure while changing the checking ritual" is more precise than "increase flexibility." Precision protects both sides of the treatment: it keeps OCD work active while reducing the chance that autism-related supports are mistaken for symptoms to eliminate.

Medication questions belong with a qualified prescriber. This book does not compare individual medicines or recommend starting, stopping, or changing a prescription. If medication is part of your care, bring the same mechanism-focused notes to that conversation: which symptoms are being targeted, what changed, what did not, and what side effects or sensory issues matter to you.

The larger principle is simple. Adaptation should not erase the treatment target, and treatment should not erase the person. A plan can be demanding where OCD requires new learning and accommodating where autism creates a different access need. Those two ideas are compatible.

Questions to Take to a Clinician

Bring examples instead of conclusions. Useful questions include: 'What makes you think this behavior is a compulsion rather than a regulating repetitive behavior?' 'What feared outcome or uncertainty are we targeting?' 'How are you accounting for sensory needs and developmental history?' 'Could both autism and OCD be present?' 'How will we know whether this intervention is reducing OCD rather than simply increasing my tolerance of distress from losing a useful support?'

A good assessment is not a debate you have to win. It is a process of making the evidence visible. You can help by naming the sequence precisely: what happened, what you thought or sensed, what you did, what you hoped the act would change, and what happened next. That gives a clinician something more useful than a checklist score alone.

Try the Four-Clue Overlap Map

Choose one example of intervention choice. On one page, make four headings: Trigger, Function, Interruption, History. Under Trigger, record what came first. Under Function, record what the behavior was meant to change. Under Interruption, record the kind of distress that appears if you stop. Under History, record when the pattern first appeared and whether it has changed. Add a final line called 'What I am not sure about.' That last line is often the most useful one to bring to assessment.

In a Nutshell

The visible behavior is the beginning of the question, not the answer. For intervention choice, look at trigger, function, interruption, and history before assigning meaning. Autism-related repetition can be valuable, regulating, pleasurable, or stabilizing. OCD compulsions are typically recruited into a cycle of threat, doubt, or rule-driven relief. Some experiences sit between those descriptions, and some people have both conditions. Your task is not to diagnose yourself from one clue. It is to build a clearer account of what is happening so the right professional questions can be asked.

References

National Institute of Mental Health. (n.d.-a). Autism spectrum disorder. https://www.nimh.nih.gov/health/publications/autism-spectrum-disorder

National Institute of Mental Health. (n.d.-b). Obsessive-compulsive disorder. https://www.nimh.nih.gov/health/topics/obsessive-compulsive-disorder-ocd

Cath, D. C., Ran, N., Smit, J. H., van Balkom, A. J. L. M., & Comijs, H. C. (2008). Symptom overlap between autism spectrum disorder, generalized social anxiety disorder and obsessive-compulsive disorder in adults: A preliminary case-controlled study. Psychopathology, 41(2), 101-110. https://pubmed.ncbi.nlm.nih.gov/18033980/

Santore, L. A., Gerber, A. H., Gioia, A. N., Bianchi, R., Talledo, F., Peris, T. S., & Lerner, M. D. (2020). Felt but not seen: Observed restricted repetitive behaviors are associated with self-report but not parent-report obsessive-compulsive disorder symptoms in youth with autism. Autism, 24(4), 983-994. https://pmc.ncbi.nlm.nih.gov/articles/PMC7337249/

Long, H. A., Rodgers, J., & South, M. (2024). 'Autism is the arena and OCD is the lion': Autistic adults' experiences of co-occurring obsessive-compulsive disorder. Autism. https://pmc.ncbi.nlm.nih.gov/articles/PMC11497754/

Wikramanayake, W. N. M., Mandy, W., Shahper, S., Kaur, S., Kolli, S., Osman, S., Reid, J., Jefferies-Sewell, K., & Fineberg, N. A. (2018). Autism spectrum disorders in adult outpatients with obsessive compulsive disorder in the UK. International Journal of Psychiatry in Clinical Practice, 22(1), 54-62. https://pubmed.ncbi.nlm.nih.gov/28705096/

Meier, S. M., Petersen, L., Schendel, D. E., Mattheisen, M., Mortensen, P. B., & Mors, O. (2015). Obsessive-compulsive disorder

and autism spectrum disorders: Longitudinal and offspring risk. PLOS ONE, 10(11), e0141703. https://pubmed.ncbi.nlm.nih.gov/26558765/

Russell, A. J., Jassi, A., Fullana, M. A., Mack, H., Johnston, K., Heyman, I., Murphy, D. G., & Mataix-Cols, D. (2013). Cognitive behavior therapy for comorbid obsessive-compulsive disorder in high-functioning autism spectrum disorders: A randomized controlled trial. Depression and Anxiety, 30(8), 697-708. https://pubmed.ncbi.nlm.nih.gov/23389964/

Flygare, O., Andersson, E., Ringberg, H., Hellstadius, K., Edbacken, J., Enander, J., Ljotsson, B., Mataix-Cols, D., & Serlachius, E. (2020). Adapted cognitive behavior therapy for obsessive-compulsive disorder with co-occurring autism spectrum disorder: A clinical effectiveness study. Autism, 24(1), 190-199. https://pubmed.ncbi.nlm.nih.gov/31187645/

National Institute for Health and Care Excellence. (2005, surveillance updated 2019). Obsessive-compulsive disorder and body dysmorphic disorder: Treatment (CG31). https://www.nice.org.uk/guidance/cg31

Chapter 13 Prepare for Assessment

Theo arrives at an appointment with 11 pages of examples. The useful part turns out to be a one-page map showing onset, trigger, purpose, interruption response, and time cost. The outside view is simple: repetition. The inside story is not. A movement, question, sequence, or thought can be repeated for several reasons, and those reasons matter more than the photograph of the behavior. This chapter uses a composite scenario. Theo's details are blended from common patterns described in the literature and are not a portrait of one real person.

Autism and OCD can both include repetition. Autism is defined in part by restricted or repetitive patterns of behavior, interests, or activities, while OCD involves obsessions, compulsions, or both (National Institute of Mental Health [NIMH], n.d.-a; National Institute of Mental Health [NIMH], n.d.-b). That overlap is exactly why appearance is a poor shortcut. The useful question is not simply, 'Is it repetitive?' It is, 'What job is the repetition doing?'

The Chapter Principle

Use the Four-Clue Overlap Map: trigger, function, interruption, and history. For clinical communication, an autism-related pattern may be connected with describing developmental history, sensory patterns, social-communication differences, interests, and routines. An OCD pattern is more likely when the act is recruited for describing obsessions, compulsions, avoidance, reassurance, time cost, and feared outcomes. None of these clues diagnoses anything by itself. Together they make a better clinical conversation.

Clue One Trigger

Start with what comes immediately before the behavior. A sensory demand, sudden transition, boredom, excitement, or need for focus can point toward regulation or predictability. A spike of doubt,

contamination fear, moral fear, harm image, or 'what if' question can point toward an OCD cycle. The same person can have both. The goal is to describe the sequence without deciding the label first.

Write the trigger as a camera could record it. 'The plan changed five minutes before we left' is better than 'I was triggered.' 'I noticed a thought that I might have left the stove on' is better than 'My anxiety got bad.' Concrete language lets a clinician ask the next question. Research comparing autism and OCD supports careful attention to phenomenology rather than assuming repetitive acts are equivalent (Cath et al., 2008; Santore et al., 2020).

Clue Two Function

Function means what the behavior is trying to change. Does it add useful sensation, organize attention, reduce overload, preserve a preferred pattern, or make an activity enjoyable? Those are different from trying to cancel danger, prove innocence, remove doubt, achieve a protective feeling, or satisfy a rule that says something bad will happen otherwise. In practice, mixed motives are common. You do not need a perfectly clean answer.

Ask a harder question: if there were no feared consequence at all, would you still want to do it? If the answer is yes because the act feels good, helps concentration, supports transition, or is part of a valued interest, that is information. If the answer is no, and the act feels like a tax paid to reduce threat or doubt, that is different information. Qualitative research with autistic adults who also have OCD describes how difficult and important this distinction can be (Long et al., 2024; Wikramanayake et al., 2018).

Clue Three Interruption

Interruption is not a morality test. Notice what kind of distress appears when the pattern is blocked. Sensory discomfort, disorganization, loss of focus, frustration at abrupt change, or a feeling of being

neurologically overloaded can occur around autistic routines and repetitive behavior. OCD interruption more often exposes the feared uncertainty the compulsion was managing: 'What if I did not check enough?' 'What if the contamination spreads?' 'What if this thought means I am dangerous?'

There is overlap here too. Autistic people can feel intense anxiety when a routine is interrupted, and people with OCD can describe bodily discomfort or a 'not just right' feeling rather than a clear catastrophic belief. That is why one clue never settles the question. The pattern across all four clues is more informative than any single answer.

Clue Four History

History asks when the pattern began and what else was true at the time. Autism is developmental, so a clinician assessing autism looks for a broader developmental pattern, not only current repetition. OCD can begin in childhood, adolescence, or adulthood and may wax and wane. A new ritual appearing after a period of intrusive doubt tells a different story from a lifelong preference for the same sensory input or sequence. Population and clinic studies show meaningful co-occurrence, so history should leave room for both rather than forcing an either-or answer (Meier et al., 2015; Wikramanayake et al., 2018).

If you can, collect examples from more than one age and setting. Old school reports, family recollections, childhood interests, early sensory patterns, and previous treatment responses can all be useful. Family memory is imperfect, and lack of documentation does not prove absence. Treat it as evidence to discuss, not a verdict.

A Worked Comparison

Take Theo's situation and write two competing explanations. Explanation A: the behavior is mainly connected with describing developmental history, sensory patterns, social-communication differences, interests, and routines. Explanation B: the behavior is mainly connected with describing obsessions, compulsions, avoidance, reassurance, time cost, and feared outcomes. Now ask what each explanation predicts. If A is closer, accommodation or regulation may reduce distress without requiring the person to defeat a fear. If B is closer, reducing compulsive responding to feared uncertainty may be clinically relevant. If both predictions fit at different times, co-occurrence becomes a serious possibility.

This method prevents a common reasoning error: treating the name of an action as if it revealed its function. 'Checking,' 'repeating,' 'collecting,' 'researching,' and 'avoiding' are verbs, not diagnoses. A person can research a favorite topic for pleasure, research a feared disease for reassurance, or do both in the same evening. Ask what happened before, what the act was supposed to accomplish, and what happened after.

What Treatment Response Can Tell You

Treatment response is information, but it is not a home diagnostic test. ERP is an evidence-based component of CBT for OCD, and studies suggest adapted CBT can help autistic people who genuinely have co-occurring OCD (Russell et al., 2013; Flygare et al., 2020; National Institute for Health and Care Excellence [NICE], 2005/2019). That does not mean every repetitive autistic behavior should be targeted with exposure. If the target is sensory regulation, communication support, or a stable routine rather than an OCD compulsion, removing it can increase distress without treating the problem you meant to treat.

The safer principle is target accuracy. A clinician should identify the feared prediction or compulsive rule before asking you to resist a behavior as part of ERP. Adaptations may include clearer structure, concrete language, slower pacing, attention to sensory needs, and explicit differentiation between OCD goals and autism-related supports. If treatment repeatedly feels aimed at the wrong mechanism,

bring that observation back to the clinician rather than trying to push through on principle.

What Appearance Gets Wrong

A quick label can hide mixed functions. With clinical communication, three mistakes are especially common. The first is assuming that visible anxiety proves OCD. A disrupted autistic routine or sensory overload can produce intense anxiety without a compulsion being present. The second is assuming that enjoyment rules OCD out. A person can feel temporary relief after a compulsion, and relief can be mistaken for preference. The third is assuming that a behavior has one function forever. A lifelong routine can later become entangled with OCD, or a person can begin using a familiar autistic behavior as part of a new threat-reduction rule.

For that reason, describe episodes rather than traits whenever you can. Instead of writing, "I always do this because I am autistic," record one recent example. Instead of writing, "This is definitely OCD," record the feared possibility, the rule, and what the behavior was supposed to prevent. Good differential assessment is built from patterns across examples. It is also allowed to end with more than one explanation.

Turn Notes Into Clinical Evidence

People often prepare for assessment by collecting everything. The result can be a long document that is emotionally important but hard to use in a time-limited appointment. The better strategy is selection.

Choose three examples that look similar from the outside but feel different inside. For each, write the trigger, function, interruption response, and history in a few lines. Add the amount of time the pattern takes, the degree of interference, and what you have already tried. If you have one example from childhood and one from the present, include both.

Then add two questions you want the assessor to answer. "Could this be a sensory regulation pattern rather than a compulsion?" is better than "Do I have autism?" because it points to evidence. "What makes this checking OCD rather than a routine?" invites the clinician to explain the formulation. A good assessment should be able to tolerate that level of specificity.

You can also bring previous reports, but do not assume an old label settles the current question. Diagnostic history is evidence, not a veto. The aim of preparation is to reduce the amount of interpretation you have to do in the room and increase the amount of observable detail the clinician has to work with.

Questions to Take to a Clinician

Bring examples instead of conclusions. Useful questions include: 'What makes you think this behavior is a compulsion rather than a regulating repetitive behavior?' 'What feared outcome or uncertainty are we targeting?' 'How are you accounting for sensory needs and developmental history?' 'Could both autism and OCD be present?' 'How will we know whether this intervention is reducing OCD rather than simply increasing my tolerance of distress from losing a useful support?'

A good assessment is not a debate you have to win. It is a process of making the evidence visible. You can help by naming the sequence precisely: what happened, what you thought or sensed, what you did, what you hoped the act would change, and what happened next. That gives a clinician something more useful than a checklist score alone.

Try the Four-Clue Overlap Map

Choose one example of clinical communication. On one page, make four headings: Trigger, Function, Interruption, History. Under Trigger, record what came first. Under Function, record what the behavior was meant to change. Under Interruption, record the kind of distress that appears if you stop. Under History, record when the pattern first appeared and whether it has changed. Add a final line called 'What I am not sure about.' That last line is often the most useful one to bring to assessment.

Principles to Remember

The visible behavior is the beginning of the question, not the answer. For clinical communication, look at trigger, function, interruption, and history before assigning meaning. Autism-related repetition can be valuable, regulating, pleasurable, or stabilizing. OCD compulsions are typically recruited into a cycle of threat, doubt, or rule-driven relief. Some experiences sit between those descriptions, and some people have both conditions. Your task is not to diagnose yourself from one clue. It is to build a clearer account of what is happening so the right professional questions can be asked.

References

National Institute of Mental Health. (n.d.-a). Autism spectrum disorder. https://www.nimh.nih.gov/health/publications/autism-spectrum-disorder

National Institute of Mental Health. (n.d.-b). Obsessive-compulsive disorder. https://www.nimh.nih.gov/health/topics/obsessive-compulsive-disorder-ocd

Cath, D. C., Ran, N., Smit, J. H., van Balkom, A. J. L. M., & Comijs, H. C. (2008). Symptom overlap between autism spectrum disorder, generalized social anxiety disorder and obsessive-compulsive disorder in adults: A preliminary case-controlled study. Psychopathology, 41(2), 101-110. https://pubmed.ncbi.nlm.nih.gov/18033980/

Santore, L. A., Gerber, A. H., Gioia, A. N., Bianchi, R., Talledo, F., Peris, T. S., & Lerner, M. D. (2020). Felt but not seen: Observed restricted repetitive behaviors are associated with self-report but not parent-report obsessive-compulsive disorder symptoms in youth with autism. Autism, 24(4), 983-994. https://pmc.ncbi.nlm.nih.gov/articles/PMC7337249/

Long, H. A., Rodgers, J., & South, M. (2024). 'Autism is the arena and OCD is the lion': Autistic adults' experiences of co-occurring obsessive-compulsive disorder. Autism. https://pmc.ncbi.nlm.nih.gov/articles/PMC11497754/

Wikramanayake, W. N. M., Mandy, W., Shahper, S., Kaur, S., Kolli, S., Osman, S., Reid, J., Jefferies-Sewell, K., & Fineberg, N. A. (2018). Autism spectrum disorders in adult outpatients with obsessive compulsive disorder in the UK. International Journal of Psychiatry in Clinical Practice, 22(1), 54-62. https://pubmed.ncbi.nlm.nih.gov/28705096/

Meier, S. M., Petersen, L., Schendel, D. E., Mattheisen, M., Mortensen, P. B., & Mors, O. (2015). Obsessive-compulsive disorder and autism spectrum disorders: Longitudinal and offspring risk. PLOS ONE, 10(11), e0141703. https://pubmed.ncbi.nlm.nih.gov/26558765/

Russell, A. J., Jassi, A., Fullana, M. A., Mack, H., Johnston, K., Heyman, I., Murphy, D. G., & Mataix-Cols, D. (2013). Cognitive behavior therapy for comorbid obsessive-compulsive disorder in high-functioning autism spectrum disorders: A randomized controlled trial. Depression and Anxiety, 30(8), 697-708. https://pubmed.ncbi.nlm.nih.gov/23389964/

Flygare, O., Andersson, E., Ringberg, H., Hellstadius, K., Edbacken, J., Enander, J., Ljotsson, B., Mataix-Cols, D., & Serlachius, E. (2020). Adapted cognitive behavior therapy for obsessive-compulsive disorder with co-occurring autism spectrum disorder: A clinical effectiveness study. Autism, 24(1), 190-199. https://pubmed.ncbi.nlm.nih.gov/31187645/

National Institute for Health and Care Excellence. (2005, surveillance updated 2019). Obsessive-compulsive disorder and body dysmorphic disorder: Treatment (CG31). https://www.nice.org.uk/guidance/cg31

Chapter 14 What Other People Can See

An observer can report what happened, but not automatically why it happened. Grace's partner can see that she returns to the front door three times, but cannot see the silent sentence she repeats each time or the feared responsibility she is trying to neutralize. The outside view is simple: repetition. The inside story is not. A movement, question, sequence, or thought can be repeated for several reasons, and those reasons matter more than the photograph of the behavior. This chapter uses a composite scenario. Grace's details are blended from common patterns described in the literature and are not a portrait of one real person.

Autism and OCD can both include repetition. Autism is defined in part by restricted or repetitive patterns of behavior, interests, or activities, while OCD involves obsessions, compulsions, or both (National Institute of Mental Health [NIMH], n.d.-a; National Institute of Mental Health [NIMH], n.d.-b). That overlap is exactly why appearance is a poor shortcut. The useful question is not simply, 'Is it repetitive?' It is, 'What job is the repetition doing?'

The Chapter Principle

Use the Four-Clue Overlap Map: trigger, function, interruption, and history. For outside observation, an autism-related pattern may be connected with others may notice routines, sensory patterns, communication differences, or focused interests without knowing their internal function. An OCD pattern is more likely when the act is recruited for others may notice checking, avoidance, reassurance, or repeated questions without hearing the obsession or mental ritual behind them. None of these clues diagnoses anything by itself. Together they make a better clinical conversation.

Clue One Trigger

Start with what comes immediately before the behavior. A sensory demand, sudden transition, boredom, excitement, or need for focus can point toward regulation or predictability. A spike of doubt, contamination fear, moral fear, harm image, or 'what if' question can point toward an OCD cycle. The same person can have both. The goal is to describe the sequence without deciding the label first.

Write the trigger as a camera could record it. 'The plan changed five minutes before we left' is better than 'I was triggered.' 'I noticed a thought that I might have left the stove on' is better than 'My anxiety got bad.' Concrete language lets a clinician ask the next question. Research comparing autism and OCD supports careful attention to phenomenology rather than assuming repetitive acts are equivalent (Cath et al., 2008; Santore et al., 2020).

Clue Two Function

Function means what the behavior is trying to change. Does it add useful sensation, organize attention, reduce overload, preserve a preferred pattern, or make an activity enjoyable? Those are different from trying to cancel danger, prove innocence, remove doubt, achieve a protective feeling, or satisfy a rule that says something bad will happen otherwise. In practice, mixed motives are common. You do not need a perfectly clean answer.

Ask a harder question: if there were no feared consequence at all, would you still want to do it? If the answer is yes because the act feels good, helps concentration, supports transition, or is part of a valued interest, that is information. If the answer is no, and the act feels like a tax paid to reduce threat or doubt, that is different information. Qualitative research with autistic adults who also have OCD describes how difficult and important this distinction can be (Long et al., 2024; Wikramanayake et al., 2018).

Clue Three Interruption

Interruption is not a morality test. Notice what kind of distress appears when the pattern is blocked. Sensory discomfort, disorganization, loss of focus, frustration at abrupt change, or a feeling of being neurologically overloaded can occur around autistic routines and repetitive behavior. OCD interruption more often exposes the feared uncertainty the compulsion was managing: 'What if I did not check enough?' 'What if the contamination spreads?' 'What if this thought means I am dangerous?'

There is overlap here too. Autistic people can feel intense anxiety when a routine is interrupted, and people with OCD can describe bodily discomfort or a 'not just right' feeling rather than a clear catastrophic belief. That is why one clue never settles the question. The pattern across all four clues is more informative than any single answer.

Clue Four History

History asks when the pattern began and what else was true at the time. Autism is developmental, so a clinician assessing autism looks for a broader developmental pattern, not only current repetition. OCD can begin in childhood, adolescence, or adulthood and may wax and wane. A new ritual appearing after a period of intrusive doubt tells a different story from a lifelong preference for the same sensory input or sequence. Population and clinic studies show meaningful co-occurrence, so history should leave room for both rather than forcing an either-or answer (Meier et al., 2015; Wikramanayake et al., 2018).

If you can, collect examples from more than one age and setting. Old school reports, family recollections, childhood interests, early sensory patterns, and previous treatment responses can all be useful. Family memory is imperfect, and lack of documentation does not prove absence. Treat it as evidence to discuss, not a verdict.

A Worked Comparison

Take Grace's situation and write two competing explanations. Explanation A: the behavior is mainly connected with others may notice routines, sensory patterns, communication differences, or focused interests without knowing their internal function. Explanation B: the behavior is mainly connected with others may notice checking, avoidance, reassurance, or repeated questions without hearing the obsession or mental ritual behind them. Now ask what each explanation predicts. If A is closer, accommodation or regulation may reduce distress without requiring the person to defeat a fear. If B is closer, reducing compulsive responding to feared uncertainty may be clinically relevant. If both predictions fit at different times, co-occurrence becomes a serious possibility.

This method prevents a common reasoning error: treating the name of an action as if it revealed its function. 'Checking,' 'repeating,' 'collecting,' 'researching,' and 'avoiding' are verbs, not diagnoses. A person can research a favorite topic for pleasure, research a feared disease for reassurance, or do both in the same evening. Ask what happened before, what the act was supposed to accomplish, and what happened after.

What Treatment Response Can Tell You

Treatment response is information, but it is not a home diagnostic test. ERP is an evidence-based component of CBT for OCD, and studies suggest adapted CBT can help autistic people who genuinely have co-occurring OCD (Russell et al., 2013; Flygare et al., 2020; National Institute for Health and Care Excellence [NICE], 2005/2019). That does not mean every repetitive autistic behavior should be targeted with exposure. If the target is sensory regulation, communication support, or a stable routine rather than an OCD compulsion, removing it can increase distress without treating the problem you meant to treat.

The safer principle is target accuracy. A clinician should identify the feared prediction or compulsive rule before asking you to resist a behavior as part of ERP. Adaptations may include clearer structure, concrete language, slower pacing, attention to sensory needs, and explicit differentiation between OCD goals and autism-related supports. If treatment repeatedly feels aimed at the wrong mechanism, bring that observation back to the clinician rather than trying to push through on principle.

What Appearance Gets Wrong

A quick label can hide mixed functions. With outside observation, three mistakes are especially common. The first is assuming that visible anxiety proves OCD. A disrupted autistic routine or sensory overload can produce intense anxiety without a compulsion being present. The second is assuming that enjoyment rules OCD out. A person can feel temporary relief after a compulsion, and relief can be mistaken for preference. The third is assuming that a behavior has one function forever. A lifelong routine can later become entangled with OCD, or a person can begin using a familiar autistic behavior as part of a new threat-reduction rule.

For that reason, describe episodes rather than traits whenever you can. Instead of writing, "I always do this because I am autistic," record one recent example. Instead of writing, "This is definitely OCD," record the feared possibility, the rule, and what the behavior was supposed to prevent. Good differential assessment is built from patterns across examples. It is also allowed to end with more than one explanation.

Questions to Take to a Clinician

Bring examples instead of conclusions. Useful questions include: 'What makes you think this behavior is a compulsion rather than a regulating repetitive behavior?' 'What feared outcome or uncertainty are we targeting?' 'How are you accounting for sensory needs and developmental history?' 'Could both autism and OCD be present?' 'How will we know whether this intervention is reducing OCD rather than simply increasing my tolerance of distress from losing a useful support?'

A good assessment is not a debate you have to win. It is a process of making the evidence visible. You can help by naming the sequence precisely: what happened, what you thought or sensed, what you did, what you hoped the act would change, and what happened next. That gives a clinician something more useful than a checklist score alone.

Try the Four-Clue Overlap Map

Choose one example of outside observation. On one page, make four headings: Trigger, Function, Interruption, History. Under Trigger, record what came first. Under Function, record what the behavior was meant to change. Under Interruption, record the kind of distress that appears if you stop. Under History, record when the pattern first appeared and whether it has changed. Add a final line called 'What I am not sure about.' That last line is often the most useful one to bring to assessment.

In a Nutshell

The visible behavior is the beginning of the question, not the answer. For outside observation, look at trigger, function, interruption, and history before assigning meaning. Autism-related repetition can be valuable, regulating, pleasurable, or stabilizing. OCD compulsions are typically recruited into a cycle of threat, doubt, or rule-driven relief. Some experiences sit between those descriptions, and some people have both conditions. Your task is not to diagnose yourself from one clue. It is to build a clearer account of what is happening so the right professional questions can be asked.

References

National Institute of Mental Health. (n.d.-a). Autism spectrum disorder. https://www.nimh.nih.gov/health/publications/autism-spectrum-disorder

National Institute of Mental Health. (n.d.-b). Obsessive-compulsive disorder. https://www.nimh.nih.gov/health/topics/obsessive-compulsive-disorder-ocd

Cath, D. C., Ran, N., Smit, J. H., van Balkom, A. J. L. M., & Comijs, H. C. (2008). Symptom overlap between autism spectrum disorder, generalized social anxiety disorder and obsessive-compulsive disorder in adults: A preliminary case-controlled study. Psychopathology, 41(2), 101-110. https://pubmed.ncbi.nlm.nih.gov/18033980/

Santore, L. A., Gerber, A. H., Gioia, A. N., Bianchi, R., Talledo, F., Peris, T. S., & Lerner, M. D. (2020). Felt but not seen: Observed restricted repetitive behaviors are associated with self-report but not parent-report obsessive-compulsive disorder symptoms in youth with autism. Autism, 24(4), 983-994. https://pmc.ncbi.nlm.nih.gov/articles/PMC7337249/

Long, H. A., Rodgers, J., & South, M. (2024). 'Autism is the arena and OCD is the lion': Autistic adults' experiences of co-occurring obsessive-compulsive disorder. Autism. https://pmc.ncbi.nlm.nih.gov/articles/PMC11497754/

Wikramanayake, W. N. M., Mandy, W., Shahper, S., Kaur, S., Kolli, S., Osman, S., Reid, J., Jefferies-Sewell, K., & Fineberg, N. A. (2018). Autism spectrum disorders in adult outpatients with obsessive compulsive disorder in the UK. International Journal of Psychiatry in Clinical Practice, 22(1), 54-62. https://pubmed.ncbi.nlm.nih.gov/28705096/

Meier, S. M., Petersen, L., Schendel, D. E., Mattheisen, M., Mortensen, P. B., & Mors, O. (2015). Obsessive-compulsive disorder

and autism spectrum disorders: Longitudinal and offspring risk. PLOS ONE, 10(11), e0141703. https://pubmed.ncbi.nlm.nih.gov/26558765/

Russell, A. J., Jassi, A., Fullana, M. A., Mack, H., Johnston, K., Heyman, I., Murphy, D. G., & Mataix-Cols, D. (2013). Cognitive behavior therapy for comorbid obsessive-compulsive disorder in high-functioning autism spectrum disorders: A randomized controlled trial. Depression and Anxiety, 30(8), 697-708. https://pubmed.ncbi.nlm.nih.gov/23389964/

Flygare, O., Andersson, E., Ringberg, H., Hellstadius, K., Edbacken, J., Enander, J., Ljotsson, B., Mataix-Cols, D., & Serlachius, E. (2020). Adapted cognitive behavior therapy for obsessive-compulsive disorder with co-occurring autism spectrum disorder: A clinical effectiveness study. Autism, 24(1), 190-199. https://pubmed.ncbi.nlm.nih.gov/31187645/

National Institute for Health and Care Excellence. (2005, surveillance updated 2019). Obsessive-compulsive disorder and body dysmorphic disorder: Treatment (CG31). https://www.nice.org.uk/guidance/cg31

Chapter 15 When the Label Does Not Fit

Grace has completed generic anxiety work twice. It helped with ordinary worry but did not touch the checking loop that consumes her evenings. The outside view is simple: repetition. The inside story is not. A movement, question, sequence, or thought can be repeated for several reasons, and those reasons matter more than the photograph of the behavior. This chapter uses a composite scenario. Grace's details are blended from common patterns described in the literature and are not a portrait of one real person.

Autism and OCD can both include repetition. Autism is defined in part by restricted or repetitive patterns of behavior, interests, or activities, while OCD involves obsessions, compulsions, or both (National Institute of Mental Health [NIMH], n.d.-a; National Institute of Mental Health [NIMH], n.d.-b). That overlap is exactly why appearance is a poor shortcut. The useful question is not simply, 'Is it repetitive?' It is, 'What job is the repetition doing?'

The Chapter Principle

Use the Four-Clue Overlap Map: trigger, function, interruption, and history. For treatment mismatch, an autism-related pattern may be connected with asking whether autism-related needs were overlooked. An OCD pattern is more likely when the act is recruited for asking whether OCD was missed, undertreated, or hidden inside other explanations. None of these clues diagnoses anything by itself. Together they make a better clinical conversation.

Clue One Trigger

Start with what comes immediately before the behavior. A sensory demand, sudden transition, boredom, excitement, or need for focus can point toward regulation or predictability. A spike of doubt, contamination fear, moral fear, harm image, or 'what if' question can

point toward an OCD cycle. The same person can have both. The goal is to describe the sequence without deciding the label first.

Write the trigger as a camera could record it. 'The plan changed five minutes before we left' is better than 'I was triggered.' 'I noticed a thought that I might have left the stove on' is better than 'My anxiety got bad.' Concrete language lets a clinician ask the next question. Research comparing autism and OCD supports careful attention to phenomenology rather than assuming repetitive acts are equivalent (Cath et al., 2008; Santore et al., 2020).

Clue Two Function

Function means what the behavior is trying to change. Does it add useful sensation, organize attention, reduce overload, preserve a preferred pattern, or make an activity enjoyable? Those are different from trying to cancel danger, prove innocence, remove doubt, achieve a protective feeling, or satisfy a rule that says something bad will happen otherwise. In practice, mixed motives are common. You do not need a perfectly clean answer.

Ask a harder question: if there were no feared consequence at all, would you still want to do it? If the answer is yes because the act feels good, helps concentration, supports transition, or is part of a valued interest, that is information. If the answer is no, and the act feels like a tax paid to reduce threat or doubt, that is different information. Qualitative research with autistic adults who also have OCD describes how difficult and important this distinction can be (Long et al., 2024; Wikramanayake et al., 2018).

Clue Three Interruption

Interruption is not a morality test. Notice what kind of distress appears when the pattern is blocked. Sensory discomfort, disorganization, loss of focus, frustration at abrupt change, or a feeling of being neurologically overloaded can occur around autistic routines and

repetitive behavior. OCD interruption more often exposes the feared uncertainty the compulsion was managing: 'What if I did not check enough?' 'What if the contamination spreads?' 'What if this thought means I am dangerous?'

There is overlap here too. Autistic people can feel intense anxiety when a routine is interrupted, and people with OCD can describe bodily discomfort or a 'not just right' feeling rather than a clear catastrophic belief. That is why one clue never settles the question. The pattern across all four clues is more informative than any single answer.

Clue Four History

History asks when the pattern began and what else was true at the time. Autism is developmental, so a clinician assessing autism looks for a broader developmental pattern, not only current repetition. OCD can begin in childhood, adolescence, or adulthood and may wax and wane. A new ritual appearing after a period of intrusive doubt tells a different story from a lifelong preference for the same sensory input or sequence. Population and clinic studies show meaningful co-occurrence, so history should leave room for both rather than forcing an either-or answer (Meier et al., 2015; Wikramanayake et al., 2018).

If you can, collect examples from more than one age and setting. Old school reports, family recollections, childhood interests, early sensory patterns, and previous treatment responses can all be useful. Family memory is imperfect, and lack of documentation does not prove absence. Treat it as evidence to discuss, not a verdict.

A Worked Comparison

Take Grace's situation and write two competing explanations. Explanation A: the behavior is mainly connected with asking whether autism-related needs were overlooked. Explanation B: the behavior is mainly connected with asking whether OCD was missed, undertreated, or hidden inside other explanations. Now ask what each explanation predicts. If A is closer, accommodation or regulation may reduce distress without requiring the person to defeat a fear. If B is closer, reducing compulsive responding to feared uncertainty may be clinically relevant. If both predictions fit at different times, co-occurrence becomes a serious possibility.

This method prevents a common reasoning error: treating the name of an action as if it revealed its function. 'Checking,' 'repeating,' 'collecting,' 'researching,' and 'avoiding' are verbs, not diagnoses. A person can research a favorite topic for pleasure, research a feared disease for reassurance, or do both in the same evening. Ask what happened before, what the act was supposed to accomplish, and what happened after.

What Treatment Response Can Tell You

Treatment response is information, but it is not a home diagnostic test. ERP is an evidence-based component of CBT for OCD, and studies suggest adapted CBT can help autistic people who genuinely have co-occurring OCD (Russell et al., 2013; Flygare et al., 2020; National Institute for Health and Care Excellence [NICE], 2005/2019). That does not mean every repetitive autistic behavior should be targeted with exposure. If the target is sensory regulation, communication support, or a stable routine rather than an OCD compulsion, removing it can increase distress without treating the problem you meant to treat.

The safer principle is target accuracy. A clinician should identify the feared prediction or compulsive rule before asking you to resist a behavior as part of ERP. Adaptations may include clearer structure, concrete language, slower pacing, attention to sensory needs, and explicit differentiation between OCD goals and autism-related supports. If treatment repeatedly feels aimed at the wrong mechanism, bring that observation back to the clinician rather than trying to push through on principle.

What Appearance Gets Wrong

A quick label can hide mixed functions. With treatment mismatch, three mistakes are especially common. The first is assuming that visible anxiety proves OCD. A disrupted autistic routine or sensory overload can produce intense anxiety without a compulsion being present. The second is assuming that enjoyment rules OCD out. A person can feel temporary relief after a compulsion, and relief can be mistaken for preference. The third is assuming that a behavior has one function forever. A lifelong routine can later become entangled with OCD, or a person can begin using a familiar autistic behavior as part of a new threat-reduction rule.

For that reason, describe episodes rather than traits whenever you can. Instead of writing, "I always do this because I am autistic," record one recent example. Instead of writing, "This is definitely OCD," record the feared possibility, the rule, and what the behavior was supposed to prevent. Good differential assessment is built from patterns across examples. It is also allowed to end with more than one explanation.

Questions to Take to a Clinician

Bring examples instead of conclusions. Useful questions include: 'What makes you think this behavior is a compulsion rather than a regulating repetitive behavior?' 'What feared outcome or uncertainty are we targeting?' 'How are you accounting for sensory needs and developmental history?' 'Could both autism and OCD be present?' 'How will we know whether this intervention is reducing OCD rather than simply increasing my tolerance of distress from losing a useful support?'

A good assessment is not a debate you have to win. It is a process of making the evidence visible. You can help by naming the sequence precisely: what happened, what you thought or sensed, what you did,

what you hoped the act would change, and what happened next. That gives a clinician something more useful than a checklist score alone.

Try the Four-Clue Overlap Map

Choose one example of treatment mismatch. On one page, make four headings: Trigger, Function, Interruption, History. Under Trigger, record what came first. Under Function, record what the behavior was meant to change. Under Interruption, record the kind of distress that appears if you stop. Under History, record when the pattern first appeared and whether it has changed. Add a final line called 'What I am not sure about.' That last line is often the most useful one to bring to assessment.

Principles to Remember

The visible behavior is the beginning of the question, not the answer. For treatment mismatch, look at trigger, function, interruption, and history before assigning meaning. Autism-related repetition can be valuable, regulating, pleasurable, or stabilizing. OCD compulsions are typically recruited into a cycle of threat, doubt, or rule-driven relief. Some experiences sit between those descriptions, and some people have both conditions. Your task is not to diagnose yourself from one clue. It is to build a clearer account of what is happening so the right professional questions can be asked.

References

National Institute of Mental Health. (n.d.-a). Autism spectrum disorder. https://www.nimh.nih.gov/health/publications/autism-spectrum-disorder

National Institute of Mental Health. (n.d.-b). Obsessive-compulsive disorder. https://www.nimh.nih.gov/health/topics/obsessive-compulsive-disorder-ocd

Cath, D. C., Ran, N., Smit, J. H., van Balkom, A. J. L. M., & Comijs, H. C. (2008). Symptom overlap between autism spectrum disorder, generalized social anxiety disorder and obsessive-compulsive disorder in adults: A preliminary case-controlled study. Psychopathology, 41(2), 101-110. https://pubmed.ncbi.nlm.nih.gov/18033980/

Santore, L. A., Gerber, A. H., Gioia, A. N., Bianchi, R., Talledo, F., Peris, T. S., & Lerner, M. D. (2020). Felt but not seen: Observed restricted repetitive behaviors are associated with self-report but not parent-report obsessive-compulsive disorder symptoms in youth with autism. Autism, 24(4), 983-994. https://pmc.ncbi.nlm.nih.gov/articles/PMC7337249/

Long, H. A., Rodgers, J., & South, M. (2024). 'Autism is the arena and OCD is the lion': Autistic adults' experiences of co-occurring obsessive-compulsive disorder. Autism. https://pmc.ncbi.nlm.nih.gov/articles/PMC11497754/

Wikramanayake, W. N. M., Mandy, W., Shahper, S., Kaur, S., Kolli, S., Osman, S., Reid, J., Jefferies-Sewell, K., & Fineberg, N. A. (2018). Autism spectrum disorders in adult outpatients with obsessive compulsive disorder in the UK. International Journal of Psychiatry in Clinical Practice, 22(1), 54-62. https://pubmed.ncbi.nlm.nih.gov/28705096/

Meier, S. M., Petersen, L., Schendel, D. E., Mattheisen, M., Mortensen, P. B., & Mors, O. (2015). Obsessive-compulsive disorder and autism spectrum disorders: Longitudinal and offspring risk. PLOS ONE, 10(11), e0141703. https://pubmed.ncbi.nlm.nih.gov/26558765/

Russell, A. J., Jassi, A., Fullana, M. A., Mack, H., Johnston, K., Heyman, I., Murphy, D. G., & Mataix-Cols, D. (2013). Cognitive behavior therapy for comorbid obsessive-compulsive disorder in high-functioning autism spectrum disorders: A randomized controlled trial. Depression and Anxiety, 30(8), 697-708. https://pubmed.ncbi.nlm.nih.gov/23389964/

Flygare, O., Andersson, E., Ringberg, H., Hellstadius, K., Edbacken, J., Enander, J., Ljotsson, B., Mataix-Cols, D., & Serlachius,

E. (2020). Adapted cognitive behavior therapy for obsessive-compulsive disorder with co-occurring autism spectrum disorder: A clinical effectiveness study. Autism, 24(1), 190-199. https://pubmed.ncbi.nlm.nih.gov/31187645/

National Institute for Health and Care Excellence. (2005, surveillance updated 2019). Obsessive-compulsive disorder and body dysmorphic disorder: Treatment (CG31). https://www.nice.org.uk/guidance/cg31

Chapter 16 Build Your Overlap Map

By the time people reach assessment, they often have years of examples and no clear way to sort them. Luis stops trying to force every behavior into a single category. Instead, he maps what starts it, what it changes, what interruption feels like, and how long the pattern has been present. The outside view is simple: repetition. The inside story is not. A movement, question, sequence, or thought can be repeated for several reasons, and those reasons matter more than the photograph of the behavior. This chapter uses a composite scenario. Luis's details are blended from common patterns described in the literature and are not a portrait of one real person.

Autism and OCD can both include repetition. Autism is defined in part by restricted or repetitive patterns of behavior, interests, or activities, while OCD involves obsessions, compulsions, or both (National Institute of Mental Health [NIMH], n.d.-a; National Institute of Mental Health [NIMH], n.d.-b). That overlap is exactly why appearance is a poor shortcut. The useful question is not simply, 'Is it repetitive?' It is, 'What job is the repetition doing?'

The Chapter Principle

Use the Four-Clue Overlap Map: trigger, function, interruption, and history. For self-observation without self-diagnosis, an autism-related pattern may be connected with tracking patterns across contexts and over time. An OCD pattern is more likely when the act is recruited for bringing clear questions and examples to a qualified clinician. None of these clues diagnoses anything by itself. Together they make a better clinical conversation.

Clue One Trigger

Start with what comes immediately before the behavior. A sensory demand, sudden transition, boredom, excitement, or need for focus can

point toward regulation or predictability. A spike of doubt, contamination fear, moral fear, harm image, or 'what if' question can point toward an OCD cycle. The same person can have both. The goal is to describe the sequence without deciding the label first.

Write the trigger as a camera could record it. 'The plan changed five minutes before we left' is better than 'I was triggered.' 'I noticed a thought that I might have left the stove on' is better than 'My anxiety got bad.' Concrete language lets a clinician ask the next question. Research comparing autism and OCD supports careful attention to phenomenology rather than assuming repetitive acts are equivalent (Cath et al., 2008; Santore et al., 2020).

Clue Two Function

Function means what the behavior is trying to change. Does it add useful sensation, organize attention, reduce overload, preserve a preferred pattern, or make an activity enjoyable? Those are different from trying to cancel danger, prove innocence, remove doubt, achieve a protective feeling, or satisfy a rule that says something bad will happen otherwise. In practice, mixed motives are common. You do not need a perfectly clean answer.

Ask a harder question: if there were no feared consequence at all, would you still want to do it? If the answer is yes because the act feels good, helps concentration, supports transition, or is part of a valued interest, that is information. If the answer is no, and the act feels like a tax paid to reduce threat or doubt, that is different information. Qualitative research with autistic adults who also have OCD describes how difficult and important this distinction can be (Long et al., 2024; Wikramanayake et al., 2018).

Clue Three Interruption

Interruption is not a morality test. Notice what kind of distress appears when the pattern is blocked. Sensory discomfort, disorganization, loss

of focus, frustration at abrupt change, or a feeling of being neurologically overloaded can occur around autistic routines and repetitive behavior. OCD interruption more often exposes the feared uncertainty the compulsion was managing: 'What if I did not check enough?' 'What if the contamination spreads?' 'What if this thought means I am dangerous?'

There is overlap here too. Autistic people can feel intense anxiety when a routine is interrupted, and people with OCD can describe bodily discomfort or a 'not just right' feeling rather than a clear catastrophic belief. That is why one clue never settles the question. The pattern across all four clues is more informative than any single answer.

Clue Four History

History asks when the pattern began and what else was true at the time. Autism is developmental, so a clinician assessing autism looks for a broader developmental pattern, not only current repetition. OCD can begin in childhood, adolescence, or adulthood and may wax and wane. A new ritual appearing after a period of intrusive doubt tells a different story from a lifelong preference for the same sensory input or sequence. Population and clinic studies show meaningful co-occurrence, so history should leave room for both rather than forcing an either-or answer (Meier et al., 2015; Wikramanayake et al., 2018).

If you can, collect examples from more than one age and setting. Old school reports, family recollections, childhood interests, early sensory patterns, and previous treatment responses can all be useful. Family memory is imperfect, and lack of documentation does not prove absence. Treat it as evidence to discuss, not a verdict.

A Worked Comparison

Take Luis's situation and write two competing explanations. Explanation A: the behavior is mainly connected with tracking patterns across contexts and over time. Explanation B: the behavior is mainly connected with bringing clear questions and examples to a qualified clinician. Now ask what each explanation predicts. If A is closer, accommodation or regulation may reduce distress without requiring the person to defeat a fear. If B is closer, reducing compulsive responding to feared uncertainty may be clinically relevant. If both predictions fit at different times, co-occurrence becomes a serious possibility.

This method prevents a common reasoning error: treating the name of an action as if it revealed its function. 'Checking,' 'repeating,' 'collecting,' 'researching,' and 'avoiding' are verbs, not diagnoses. A person can research a favorite topic for pleasure, research a feared disease for reassurance, or do both in the same evening. Ask what happened before, what the act was supposed to accomplish, and what happened after.

What Treatment Response Can Tell You

Treatment response is information, but it is not a home diagnostic test. ERP is an evidence-based component of CBT for OCD, and studies suggest adapted CBT can help autistic people who genuinely have co-occurring OCD (Russell et al., 2013; Flygare et al., 2020; National Institute for Health and Care Excellence [NICE], 2005/2019). That does not mean every repetitive autistic behavior should be targeted with exposure. If the target is sensory regulation, communication support, or a stable routine rather than an OCD compulsion, removing it can increase distress without treating the problem you meant to treat.

The safer principle is target accuracy. A clinician should identify the feared prediction or compulsive rule before asking you to resist a behavior as part of ERP. Adaptations may include clearer structure, concrete language, slower pacing, attention to sensory needs, and explicit differentiation between OCD goals and autism-related supports. If treatment repeatedly feels aimed at the wrong mechanism,

bring that observation back to the clinician rather than trying to push through on principle.

What Appearance Gets Wrong

A quick label can hide mixed functions. With self-observation without self-diagnosis, three mistakes are especially common. The first is assuming that visible anxiety proves OCD. A disrupted autistic routine or sensory overload can produce intense anxiety without a compulsion being present. The second is assuming that enjoyment rules OCD out. A person can feel temporary relief after a compulsion, and relief can be mistaken for preference. The third is assuming that a behavior has one function forever. A lifelong routine can later become entangled with OCD, or a person can begin using a familiar autistic behavior as part of a new threat-reduction rule.

For that reason, describe episodes rather than traits whenever you can. Instead of writing, "I always do this because I am autistic," record one recent example. Instead of writing, "This is definitely OCD," record the feared possibility, the rule, and what the behavior was supposed to prevent. Good differential assessment is built from patterns across examples. It is also allowed to end with more than one explanation.

Questions to Take to a Clinician

Bring examples instead of conclusions. Useful questions include: 'What makes you think this behavior is a compulsion rather than a regulating repetitive behavior?' 'What feared outcome or uncertainty are we targeting?' 'How are you accounting for sensory needs and developmental history?' 'Could both autism and OCD be present?' 'How will we know whether this intervention is reducing OCD rather than simply increasing my tolerance of distress from losing a useful support?'

A good assessment is not a debate you have to win. It is a process of making the evidence visible. You can help by naming the sequence precisely: what happened, what you thought or sensed, what you did, what you hoped the act would change, and what happened next. That gives a clinician something more useful than a checklist score alone.

Try the Four-Clue Overlap Map

Choose one example of self-observation without self-diagnosis. On one page, make four headings: Trigger, Function, Interruption, History. Under Trigger, record what came first. Under Function, record what the behavior was meant to change. Under Interruption, record the kind of distress that appears if you stop. Under History, record when the pattern first appeared and whether it has changed. Add a final line called 'What I am not sure about.' That last line is often the most useful one to bring to assessment.

In a Nutshell

The visible behavior is the beginning of the question, not the answer. For self-observation without self-diagnosis, look at trigger, function, interruption, and history before assigning meaning. Autism-related repetition can be valuable, regulating, pleasurable, or stabilizing. OCD compulsions are typically recruited into a cycle of threat, doubt, or rule-driven relief. Some experiences sit between those descriptions, and some people have both conditions. Your task is not to diagnose yourself from one clue. It is to build a clearer account of what is happening so the right professional questions can be asked.

References

National Institute of Mental Health. (n.d.-a). Autism spectrum disorder. https://www.nimh.nih.gov/health/publications/autism-spectrum-disorder

National Institute of Mental Health. (n.d.-b). Obsessive-compulsive disorder. https://www.nimh.nih.gov/health/topics/obsessive-compulsive-disorder-ocd

Cath, D. C., Ran, N., Smit, J. H., van Balkom, A. J. L. M., & Comijs, H. C. (2008). Symptom overlap between autism spectrum disorder, generalized social anxiety disorder and obsessive-compulsive disorder in adults: A preliminary case-controlled study. Psychopathology, 41(2), 101-110. https://pubmed.ncbi.nlm.nih.gov/18033980/

Santore, L. A., Gerber, A. H., Gioia, A. N., Bianchi, R., Talledo, F., Peris, T. S., & Lerner, M. D. (2020). Felt but not seen: Observed restricted repetitive behaviors are associated with self-report but not parent-report obsessive-compulsive disorder symptoms in youth with autism. Autism, 24(4), 983-994. https://pmc.ncbi.nlm.nih.gov/articles/PMC7337249/

Long, H. A., Rodgers, J., & South, M. (2024). 'Autism is the arena and OCD is the lion': Autistic adults' experiences of co-occurring obsessive-compulsive disorder. Autism. https://pmc.ncbi.nlm.nih.gov/articles/PMC11497754/

Wikramanayake, W. N. M., Mandy, W., Shahper, S., Kaur, S., Kolli, S., Osman, S., Reid, J., Jefferies-Sewell, K., & Fineberg, N. A. (2018). Autism spectrum disorders in adult outpatients with obsessive compulsive disorder in the UK. International Journal of Psychiatry in Clinical Practice, 22(1), 54-62. https://pubmed.ncbi.nlm.nih.gov/28705096/

Meier, S. M., Petersen, L., Schendel, D. E., Mattheisen, M., Mortensen, P. B., & Mors, O. (2015). Obsessive-compulsive disorder and autism spectrum disorders: Longitudinal and offspring risk. PLOS ONE, 10(11), e0141703. https://pubmed.ncbi.nlm.nih.gov/26558765/

Russell, A. J., Jassi, A., Fullana, M. A., Mack, H., Johnston, K., Heyman, I., Murphy, D. G., & Mataix-Cols, D. (2013). Cognitive behavior therapy for comorbid obsessive-compulsive disorder in high-functioning autism spectrum disorders: A randomized controlled trial.

Depression and Anxiety, 30(8), 697-708. https://pubmed.ncbi.nlm.nih.gov/23389964/

Flygare, O., Andersson, E., Ringberg, H., Hellstadius, K., Edbacken, J., Enander, J., Ljotsson, B., Mataix-Cols, D., & Serlachius, E. (2020). Adapted cognitive behavior therapy for obsessive-compulsive disorder with co-occurring autism spectrum disorder: A clinical effectiveness study. Autism, 24(1), 190-199. https://pubmed.ncbi.nlm.nih.gov/31187645/

National Institute for Health and Care Excellence. (2005, surveillance updated 2019). Obsessive-compulsive disorder and body dysmorphic disorder: Treatment (CG31). https://www.nice.org.uk/guidance/cg31

Conclusion A Better Question

The question that brought you here may have sounded binary: autism or OCD? By now, the more useful question is probably more specific. What starts this pattern? What is it doing for me? What happens when it is interrupted? How long has it been part of my life?

Those questions do not produce a diagnosis on their own. They do something more practical. They separate outward appearance from internal function and create a record that can be examined with a clinician.

You may find that some patterns make sense as regulation, sensory support, focused interest, or a preference for predictability. Others may look more like intrusive doubt followed by checking, neutralizing, reassurance, avoidance, or another compulsion. Some may remain unclear. Some people will have evidence pointing toward both autism and OCD.

That is not a failure of the method. The goal was never to force every behavior into a box. The goal was to make the ambiguity more precise.

If you take one thing from this book, take the Four-Clue Overlap Map with you. Trigger. Function. Interruption. History. Bring concrete examples. Ask what mechanism a clinician thinks is operating. Ask what evidence supports that view. Ask how a treatment target was chosen.

A good next step is not a perfect label written in your own handwriting. It is a better clinical question, backed by observations that are hard to dismiss.

Appendix A The Four-Clue Overlap Map

Use one page for one behavior or mental pattern.

Trigger: What happened immediately before it? Include sensory input, a transition, boredom, excitement, an intrusive thought, doubt, a feared possibility, or a change in plan.

Function: What did you want the behavior to change? Did it add regulation, pleasure, focus, or predictability? Did it aim to prevent danger, reduce doubt, cancel a thought, prove something, or make a feared feeling go away?

Interruption: If you stop or are prevented from doing it, what kind of distress appears? Describe the distress rather than rating it only.

History: When did the pattern begin? Was something similar present in childhood? Has the reason for doing it changed over time?

Uncertainty: What still does not fit either explanation?

Appendix B Assessment Preparation Sheet

Bring three to five examples rather than a complete life history. For each example, write the Four-Clue Overlap Map in brief. Add developmental history that may be relevant to autism, and note OCD features such as intrusive unwanted thoughts, compulsive behavior, reassurance, avoidance, and time cost.

Questions you can ask include: What makes you think this is a compulsion rather than a regulating behavior? What feared outcome or uncertainty is the intervention targeting? How are sensory needs being considered? Could both conditions be present? What would make you revise the working formulation?

Glossary

Autism: A neurodevelopmental condition involving social-communication differences and restricted or repetitive patterns of behavior, interests, or activities.

Compulsion: A repetitive behavior or mental act performed according to a rule or in response to an obsession, commonly intended to reduce distress or prevent a feared event.

ERP: Exposure and response prevention, a form of CBT used for OCD that involves planned contact with feared cues or uncertainty while reducing compulsive responding.

Four-Clue Overlap Map: The framework used in this book: trigger, function, interruption, and history.

Function: The job a behavior or mental act is doing in context.

Intrusive thought: An unwanted thought, image, or urge that enters awareness. Intrusive thoughts occur broadly; in OCD they can become persistent targets of threat appraisal and compulsive response.

Obsession: In OCD, a recurrent intrusive and unwanted thought, urge, or image that causes distress or anxiety.

Repetitive behavior: An umbrella description for repeated movement, action, speech, thought, routine, or sequence. The phrase does not identify cause.

Routine: A repeated sequence that can support predictability, efficiency, comfort, or transition.

Special interest: An intense or focused interest that may be absorbing, pleasurable, identity-relevant, or expertise-building.

Stim: Informal shorthand for self-stimulatory behavior, often used for repetitive movement, sound, or sensory activity associated with regulation, expression, or sensory input.

About the Author

Evie Dove Huynh writes plain-language guides for people caught between two possible explanations for what they're experiencing.

Her books grew out of a simple observation: most self-help assumes you already know what you're dealing with. The shelves are full of books about OCD, about autism, about burnout, and almost nothing for the person still trying to work out which one applies to them. That gap is where people lose years.

She writes for the reader in that gap. Every book draws on current peer-reviewed research, cites its sources so you can check them, and explains the distinctions in language you could repeat to a doctor. She doesn't diagnose, and she's clear about that throughout. What she offers is the vocabulary and the questions to take to someone who can.

Evie writes full-time and reads more clinical literature than is strictly healthy.

About the Series

Two conditions. One set of symptoms. Completely different answers.

Some of the most consequential questions in mental health and neurodivergence come down to telling apart two things that look almost identical from the inside. Is this OCD or is it autism? A meltdown or a panic attack? Burnout, or depression? ADHD, or something closer to bipolar?

The distinctions matter because they can change what kind of support is useful. Yet almost every book on the shelf begins after the question is settled. This series begins before it.

Each volume takes one pair of commonly confused conditions and lays them side by side: what each is, how they differ in ways you can observe, why the same intervention may fit one pattern better than another, and what to say to a clinician to get the question properly examined.

These books do not diagnose. No book can. What they offer is a clearer picture of what you might be looking at, and the language to take it to someone who can help.

References

National Institute of Mental Health. (n.d.-a). Autism spectrum disorder. https://www.nimh.nih.gov/health/publications/autism-spectrum-disorder

National Institute of Mental Health. (n.d.-b). Obsessive-compulsive disorder. https://www.nimh.nih.gov/health/topics/obsessive-compulsive-disorder-ocd

Wikramanayake, W. N. M., Mandy, W., Shahper, S., Kaur, S., Kolli, S., Osman, S., Reid, J., Jefferies-Sewell, K., & Fineberg, N. A. (2018). Autism spectrum disorders in adult outpatients with obsessive compulsive disorder in the UK. International Journal of Psychiatry in Clinical Practice, 22(1), 54-62. https://pubmed.ncbi.nlm.nih.gov/28705096/

Meier, S. M., Petersen, L., Schendel, D. E., Mattheisen, M., Mortensen, P. B., & Mors, O. (2015). Obsessive-compulsive disorder and autism spectrum disorders: Longitudinal and offspring risk. PLOS ONE, 10(11), e0141703. https://pubmed.ncbi.nlm.nih.gov/26558765/

Russell, A. J., Jassi, A., Fullana, M. A., Mack, H., Johnston, K., Heyman, I., Murphy, D. G., & Mataix-Cols, D. (2013). Cognitive behavior therapy for comorbid obsessive-compulsive disorder in high-functioning autism spectrum disorders: A randomized controlled trial. Depression and Anxiety, 30(8), 697-708. https://pubmed.ncbi.nlm.nih.gov/23389964/

Flygare, O., Andersson, E., Ringberg, H., Hellstadius, K., Edbacken, J., Enander, J., Ljotsson, B., Mataix-Cols, D., & Serlachius, E. (2020). Adapted cognitive behavior therapy for obsessive-compulsive disorder with co-occurring autism spectrum disorder: A clinical effectiveness study. Autism, 24(1), 190-199. https://pubmed.ncbi.nlm.nih.gov/31187645/

Long, H. A., Rodgers, J., & South, M. (2024). 'Autism is the arena and OCD is the lion': Autistic adults' experiences of co-occurring obsessive-compulsive disorder. Autism. https://pmc.ncbi.nlm.nih.gov/articles/PMC11497754/

National Institute for Health and Care Excellence. (2005, surveillance updated 2019). Obsessive-compulsive disorder and body dysmorphic disorder: Treatment (CG31). https://www.nice.org.uk/guidance/cg31

Cath, D. C., Ran, N., Smit, J. H., van Balkom, A. J. L. M., & Comijs, H. C. (2008). Symptom overlap between autism spectrum disorder, generalized social anxiety disorder and obsessive-compulsive disorder in adults: A preliminary case-controlled study. Psychopathology, 41(2), 101-110. https://pubmed.ncbi.nlm.nih.gov/18033980/

Santore, L. A., Gerber, A. H., Gioia, A. N., Bianchi, R., Talledo, F., Peris, T. S., & Lerner, M. D. (2020). Felt but not seen: Observed restricted repetitive behaviors are associated with self-report but not parent-report obsessive-compulsive disorder symptoms in youth with autism. Autism, 24(4), 983-994. https://pmc.ncbi.nlm.nih.gov/articles/PMC7337249/

www.ingramcontent.com/pod-product-compliance
Lightning Source LLC
LaVergne TN
LVHW010727061126
851857LV00014B/1374
9781911838630